GEORGE ELIOT'S POETRY

Kathleen Phythian
55 Rodney St.

March 2004 — working very hard
so near and yet so far.
Loneliness is so very painful
Treebeard nowhere to be found
Am losing sight of that light
at the end of the tunnell.

Companions —

Jack e Laddie e Lady e Scampi
my walks with them is all that's
keeping me going. x

Blessed Be.

GEORGE ELIOT'S POETRY

AND

OTHER STUDIES

BY

ROSE ELIZABETH CLEVELAND

University Press of the Pacific
Honolulu, Hawaii

George Eliot's Poetry and Other Studies

by
Rose Elizabeth Cleveland

ISBN: 1-4102-0588-6

Reprinted from the 1885 edition

University Press of the Pacific
Honolulu, Hawaii
http://www.universitypressofthepacific.com

To My Countrywomen

THESE ESSAYS, SOME OF WHICH WERE ORIGINALLY PREPARED
FOR USE IN SCHOOLS AND COLLEGES, ARE NOW
AFFECTIONATELY AND RESPECT-
FULLY DEDICATED.

R. E. C.

CONTENTS.

GEORGE ELIOT'S POETRY.

I.

A GENUINE poem is almost certain of recognition, as
such, in the long run. If verse contains poetry, that
poetry makes itself felt, whatever blemishes the verse, as
verse, may have ; but if dint of argument alone brings
us to acknowledge faultless verse a poem, like Galileo, in
the moment of recantation, we shall mutter to ourselves our
former and unrecanted conviction. Choose, for example,
any Paris to arbitrate between " Aurora Leigh" and " The
Spanish Gypsy," and which will win the golden apple ? If
Paris is at all able to tell black from white, he will at once
perceive the " points" of which the " Gypsy" is possessed
and of which " Aurora" is destitute. He will discover in
the pages of George Eliot superlatives enough. Their color
and glow, their vigor, their passion, their nobility of sentiment, their perfection of pathos, the sustained movement
of the story, its tragic and worthy *dénouement*, its perfect
prosody, its successful unities, and its everywhere-pervading
atmosphere of ethical sublimity—all these will compare
with " Aurora" to " Aurora's" disadvantage. And yet,
and yet—how is it ?—" Aurora" gets the apple ! Perhaps
poor Paris can only stammer forth, in answer to the question, What in " Aurora" more excellent than in the
" Gypsy" establishes her claim to the prize ?—the unan-

swering answer, "*Je ne sais quoi.*" Paris knows that by
the one he is impressed, stirred, uplifted ; and that the
other, with its high morality, and rare knowledge, and brilliant diction, falls cold upon his ear ; in short, whether he
comprehends it or not, it is the poetry in " Aurora" and
the lack of it in the " Gypsy" which compels his decision.

What's in a name ? A rose by any other name might
smell as sweet ; but a lily, if rechristened rose, would never
diffuse the rose's odor, nor gain, in addition to its own spotless perfections, the deep-hearted sorcery of that enchanting, crumpled wonder, which we thrill in touching, as if
it, too, had nerves, and blood, and a human heart—a rose !
So prose can never become poetry by bearing its name.   Ad-
ventitious circumstances—personal distinction, dazzling success in other fields, the influence of sympathetic and powerful friends—may cause something admirable as prose to
pass, for the moment, as poetry.   But the sure judgment
of time reverses such opinions, and prose continues prose,
and poetry remains forever uncounterfeited.

II.

I come at once to the consideration of George Eliot's
verse in the mention of two qualities which it seems to me
to lack, and which I hold to be essentials of poetry.

The first of these two qualities has to do with form, and
is a property, if not the whole, of the outside, that which
affects and (if anything could do this) stops with the senses.
Yet here, as elsewhere in this department of criticism, it is

difficult to be exact. I ask myself, Is it her prosody? and am obliged to find it faultless as Pope's. There is never in her metres a syllable too much or too little. Mrs. Browning's metre is often slovenly, her rhymes are often false. Yet, explain it who will, Elizabeth Browning's verse has always poetry and music, which George Eliot's lacks.

What was work to write is work to read. Ruskin's dictum— "No great intellectual thing was ever done by great effort"—I suspect to be wholly true, and that it is pre-eminently true in the production of poetry. Poetry must be the natural manner of the poet, and can never be assumed. I do not mean by this to ignore the aids which study gives to genius; I only mean to say that no mere labor and culture can simulate poetic fire, or atone for its absence. George Eliot puts her wealth of message into the mould of poetic form by continuous effort. No secret of hydraulics could cause a dewdrop to hang upon a rose-leaf in a cube. Her torrents of thought were predestined to a cubical deliverance. Never was the Calvinistic dilemma more intrusive. Her free will cannot squeeze them spherical.

George Eliot's prose carries easily its enormous burdens of concentrated gift. It is like the incomparable trained elephants of Eastern monarchs, which bear at once every treasure—the iron of agriculture, the gem of royalty; and in its cumbrous momentum it out-distances all competitors. But poesy should betray no burdens. Its rider should sit lightly, with no hint of spur. It should sport along its course and reach its goal unwearied.

The born poet has no agony in the deliverance of his song. The uttering is to him that soothing balm which

the utterance is to his reader. Burns said, " My passions
when once lighted raged like so many devils till they got
vent in rhyme ; and then the conning over my verses, like
a spell, soothed all into quiet." But where will one find a
lullaby in George Eliot's verses ?

Poets do, indeed, learn in suffering what they teach in
song ; but the singing quiets the suffering. It is the weeping, not the tear wept, that gives relief. Mrs. Browning
makes no secret of the headache.

> " If heads that hold a rhythmic thought must ache perforce,
> Then I, for one, choose headaches."

In a private letter she writes : " I have not shrunk from
any amount of labor where labor could do anything."
Where labor could do anything ! There it is !

George Eliot has been said to possess Shakespearian
qualities. Perhaps just here, in the relation of manner to
matter, is seen her greatest resemblance and greatest difference. No writer, all concede, ever carried and delivered
so much as Shakespeare. Never was human utterance so
packed with wealthy meaning, so loaded with all things
that can be thought or felt, inferred or dreamed, as his.
And it all comes with gush and rush, or with gentle, mur-
muring flow, just as it can come, just as it must come. He
takes no trouble, and he gives none. From one of his plays,
replete with his incomparable wit, wisdom, and conceit, you
emerge as from an ocean bath, exhilarated by the tossing of
billows whose rough embrace dissolves to tenderest caress,
yet carries in itself hints of central fire, of utmost horizon,
of contact with things in heaven and earth undreamt of in
our philosophy. You come from one of George Eliot's

poems as from a Turkish bath of latest science and refine-ment,—appreciative of benefit, but so battered, beaten, and disjointed as to need repose before you can be conscious of refreshment.

The irony of fate spares not one shining mark. George Eliot cared most to have the name of poet. But her gait betrays her in the borrowed robe. It is as if the parish priest should insist on wearing in his desk my lady's evening costume. It is too much and not enough. He cannot achieve my lady's trick which causes the queenly train to float behind her like the smoke-plume of a gliding engine. He steps on it and stumbles. You step on it and fall. On my lady it is never in the way; on His Rever-ence it is always so. Yet he will preach in it! " There are," writes Mrs. Browning to R. H. Horne, " Mr. ——, Mr. ——, Lord ——, and one or two others who have education and natural ability enough to be anything in the world except poets, and who choose to be poets in spite of nature and their stars, to say nothing of gods, men, and critical columns."

III.

A second quality which George Eliot's poetry lacks is internal and intrinsic, pertaining to matter rather than manner, though, as will be suggested later on, standing, perhaps, in the relation to manner of cause to effect. It is that, indeed, which all her works lack, but which prose, as prose, can get along without ; call it what you will, faith or transcendentalism ; I prefer to define it negatively as the *antipode of agnosticism.*

No capable student of her works but must admit the existence of this deficiency. Everywhere and in all things it is apparent. Between all her lines is written the stern, self-imposed thus far and no farther. Her noblest characters move, majestic and sad, up to a—stone-wall ! There is no need that argument be brought to establish this proposition. It demands—nay, admits of, no proof, for it is self-evident.

The question which concerns us here is simply, What has this fact to do with George Eliot's poetry ?

I answer, Much, every way. Herein, indeed, is matter. But my suspicions must not be disclosed in their full heterodoxy. I venture, however, to affirm that agnosticism can never exist in true poetry. Let verse have every quality which delights sense, captivates intellect, and stirs the heart, yet lack that ray which, coming from a sun beyond our system, reaches, blends with, vivifies, and assures the intimation of and longing for immortality in man —lacking this, you have not poetry.

It is the necessity of the poet, his *raison d'être*, to meet and join the moving of men's minds toward the hereafter. For all minds tend thither. The dullest mortal spirit must at times grope restlessly and expectantly in the outer darkness for something beyond ; and this something must exist, will exist, in a true poem. It need not be defined as Heaven, or Paradise, or Hades, or Nirvâna ; but we must not be confronted with silence ; there must be in some way recognition of and sympathy with this deepest yearning of the soul. Many a one, not knowing what, not seeing where, but trusting in somewhat and trusting in some-where, has been a poet and an inspiration to his race. The simplest bead-telling Margaret is appeased with the creedless faith of her Faust, though it be told in " phrases slightly different" from the parish priest's. Faust, the lore-crammed, the knowledge-sated, yet feels the unseen, and longs and trusts. His proud will brings no cold, impenetrable extin-guisher to place upon this leaping flame of spirit, which sends its groping ray far beyond his finite horizon, ever moving, moving in its search ; because he feels assurance of the existence of the something toward which it moves.

George Eliot, confronted by Margaret's question, answers sadly, with submission born of a proud ignorance, " I do not know. My feeling that there is something somewhere is, itself, unaccountable, and proves nothing. I simply do— not—know. I will not conjecture. It is idle and imperti-nent to guess. There is that of which you and I both do know, because we have experience of it. Of this only will I speak. All else is but verbiage. We stop here."

And she stops here, before a great stone-wall, higher than we can see over, thicker than we can measure, so cold that we recoil at the touch. There is no getting any farther. It is the very end.

Now, this can never be poetry ; for the poet must ever open and widen our horizon. He need not be on the wing, but his wings must be in sight. He need not—nay, he must not, deal with man-made creeds and dogmas. He need not deal with ethics even. Homer knows nothing of most of George Eliot's sweet humanities, and confuses shockingly all things which, since his poor day, have come to be catalogued under the heads of virtue and vice. His deities make merry over the cripple among them, and spend most of their time meditating guiles concerning each other, and each other's favorites among men. Humanity is the football for their game. They, the relentless, cruel immortals, are to be come up with if mortal may ; to be propitiated if mortal must. Nowhere is there any trace of conscience, nowhere any sense of sin. As to the moralities of human life, the duties of man to man, these Homeric Rob Roys found themselves amply sufficed with

> " . . . the simple plan
> That they should take who had the power,
> And they should keep who can."

Yet among all there is a boundless belief in a beyond. The imagination and anticipation of existence comes never to an end. The future is, indeed, unknown, since he who enters may not return from Hades. Yet it is vastly, vaguely certain. A multitude of immortals of infinite power and irresistible beauty surround and have continually to do with mortal men, and for each man there is some chance of winning from these immortals the gift of godhood. All expands and extends. There is no end-all, no be-all. Hence, without morality or goodness, we have poetry.

In Heine we have shocking jests and fearful impieties, but never sincere agnosticism. He believed all, and denied all. He threw away with one hand what he clasped with the other. " Lying, corpse-like, upon the barren sand by the grovelling, heaving sea, which is dipped up by the gray and formless cloud-daughters of the air, in tedious, ceaseless rise and fall (so like his own life !), he still sees the luminous aspect of a far-away perfection, in whose heavenly beauty his spirit has found the inspiration that carries it straight, like a bird, to heaven's gate." * The ilse, evanished from the waters, where prayers are said and church-bells ring, lies in the depths of his own sea-soul. Ever and anon the angel-face of the little dead Veronica woos and wins him to purity and peace.

Byron's negatives amount to an affirmative. Amid all his personal misery and assurance that

> " Whatever thou hast been,
> 'Twere something better not to be,"

he, after all, speaks only for himself. For those who care for that sort of thing there is a paradise, heaven, angels, rewards of virtue, God, etc. These things are not in his line, but he knows a good deal about them. They are, but for whom is only a matter of taste and taking the trouble.

Even the sadly carnal Swinburne predicates and carelessly hints at an over-realm. In his mournfulest negatives he arrives at certainties which put some meaning into his luxury of sound.

> " From too much love of living,
>   From hope and fear set free,
> We thank with brief thanksgiving
>   Whatever gods there be,
> That no life lives forever,
> That dead men rise up never,
> That even the weariest river
>   Winds somewhere safe to sea.

* Der Schiffbrüchige.

> " Then star nor sun shall waken,
>   Nor any change of light ;
> Nor sound of waters shaken,
>   Nor any sound or sight ;
> Nor wintry leaves, nor vernal,
> Nor days, nor things diurnal ;
> Only the sleep eternal
>   In an eternal night."

There is something quite appreciable here. It is as far
from agnosticism as it is from Christianity.

For all test one may apply to it he wins this result—
namely, that poetry, whose necessity it is to deal with
humanity in all its bearings, can never, consistently with its
mission, leave the reader merely the silence of the Sphinx
concerning the hereafter—can never return to the heavens,
aflame with sun, moon, and stars, and the milky mist of
undiscerned systems, merely the stare of stone-dead, stone-
blind eyes ! It may give him absurd fancies, wildest
dreams, sheerest nonsense, but it must give him something. It may shut him up to annihilation, but it must not
leave him to dwell with the silence of agnosticism. It
must give him, in no wise, doctrine ; not at all creed ; not,
necessarily, piety toward God or man ; but freedom, un-
limitation, a beyond, and a hereafter !

George Eliot, with brain surcharged with richest thought
and choicest, carefulest culture ; with heart to hold all
humanity, if that could save ; with tongue of men and
angels to tell the knowledge of her intellect, the charity of
her heart—yet, having not faith, becomes, for all of satisfaction that she gives the soul, but sounding brass and tinkling
cymbal ! She will not bid me hope when she herself has
no assurance of the thing hoped for. She must not speak

of faith in the unknown. She cannot be cruel, but she can be dumb ; and so her long procession of glorious thoughts, and sweet humanities, and noblest ethics, and stern renunciations, and gracious common lots, and lofty ideal lives, with their scalding tears, and bursting laughter, and flaming passion—all that enters into mortal life and time's story—makes its matchless march before our captured vision up to —the stone-wall. "And here," she says, "is *the end!*" We may accept her dictum and be brave, silent, undeceived, and undeceiving agnostics ; but, as such, we must say to her (of "The Spanish Gypsy," for instance), "This is not poetry ! It is the richest realism, presenting indubitable phenomena from which you draw, with strictest science, best deduction and inference concerning the known or the knowable. But, by virtue of all this, it is not poetry. The flattering lies and pretty guesses are not there, and will be missed. You must put them in as do the Christians, the transcendentalists, and the fools generally. The 'poet' comes from these ranks. If you will persist in this sheer stop when you reach the confines of the known, you must not attempt to pass your work off as poetry. Even pagans will not be attracted by such verse. They want and will have predication. It is not so much that you do not know—nobody knows—as that you will not guess, or dream, or fancy, to their whim ; that you will be so plainly, simply silent concerning the hereafter. Your readers will not endure that in poetry. There was John Milton, his learning as great as yours, his metres not more exact, yet nothing saves his Paradises from being theological treatises except the imagination in them, which stops not with the seen, but invades and appropriates the

unseen. This blind old Titan sees and interprets the
heavens by his inner vision. His sublime audacity of faith
aërates the ponderous craft of his verse and keeps it from
sinking into the abyss of theologic pedantry.

"Mrs. Browning, with her careless verbosity, still makes
her 'Aurora' an immortal, because both she and Aurora
believe in immortality. But your self-contained verse will
scarcely give long human life to your beloved Feldama.
However much she bids us

> '. . . Think of me as one who sees
> A light serene and strong on one sole path,
> Which she will tread till death.
>   . . . though I die alone,
> A hoary woman on the altar step,
> Cold 'mid cold ashes. That is my chief good.
> The deepest hunger of a faithful heart
> Is faithfulness. Wish me naught else'—

still your readers will persist in wishing her something else,
because they will hope and believe there is a 'good'
beyond what she calls the chief—a good toward which that
good is but a means. Her supreme renunciation will blight
her story, and men will never take it in exchange for or in
company with that of the gushing Aurora. Your sound
science and morality will win from them only silence, but
they will applaud forever such outbursts of feeling as this
of Aurora's :

> '. . . There's not a flower of spring
> That dies ere June but vaunts itself allied,
> By issue and symbol, by significance
> And correspondence, to that spirit-world
> Outside the limits of our sphere and time

> Whereto we are bound. Let poets give it voice
> With human meanings, else they miss the thought,
> And henceforth step down lower, stand confessed,
> Instructed poorly for interpreter.'

" There is that ' horse-faced' Wordsworth ! His 'drowsy, frowsy' ' Excursion' might still be gathering dust on Mr. Cottle's bookshelves but for his ' Intimations of Immortality,' which caught the ear of the unscientific people— always longing for such intimations—and forthwith he is become *poeta nascitur*. This is a very unmeaning statement :

> ' Hence, in a season of calm weather,
>   Though inland far we be,
> Our souls have sight of that immortal sea
>   Which brought us hither,
> Can in a moment travel thither
> And see the children sport upon the shore,
> And hear the mighty waters rolling evermore.'

" Yet the sentiment of these words fell in with the drift of human vagary for all time. Your noble, safe, scientific utterances will drop, dead and unregarded, beside it. It must be after many generations have been instructed in our first principles of true knowledge that your verse will be received as poetry."

Even so, Agnostic !

IV.

Perhaps these two qualities of which I have spoken—the one extrinsic, as of the body ; the other intrinsic, as of the mind ; the one sensuous, the other spiritual—may not, in the last analysis, be distinguishable, because the one is *sine*

quâ non of the other.   To use the language of one of the
agnostics, in treating of these qualities, it may come to be
" immaterial whether spirit be expressed in terms of matter,
or matter in terms of spirit."   With *poeta nascitur* it is
difficult to separate the material body from the spiritual
body, to say which is form, which spirit.   This,

> " . . . oft converse with heavenly habitants,
> Begins to cast a beam on the outward shape,
> *   *   *   *   *   *   *
> And turn it, by degrees, to the soul's essence."

George Eliot herself says, in a private letter lately given to
the public, referring to the evolution of her Dinah from
the germ sown in her mind years before by the person of
an aunt, and speaking of the unlikeness of the two, as well
as the likeness, " The difference was not merely physical.
No difference is."

No one knows better than George Eliot knew how the
spiritual body gives curve, and feature, and expression to
the material body.   Mrs. Browning herself did not more
keenly realize and everywhere acknowledge the truth that
spirit makes the form.

> " . . . Inward evermore
> To outward, so in life and so in art,
> Which still is life."

No one bows with profounder recognition to the dictum
" it is the spirit which quickeneth" than does the author of
" Adam Bede" and " The Spanish Gypsy."   It is this
which she thinks it worth while to teach, without which she
would have no heart to teach at all.   But her teaching
takes its shape from the attitude of her own soul.

To epitomize, then. George Eliot's pages are a labyrinth of wonder and beauty ; crowded with ethics lofty and pure as Plato's ; with human natures fine and fresh as Shakespeare's ; but a labyrinth in which you lose the guiding cord ! With the attitude and utterance of her spirit confronting me, I cannot allow her verse to be poetry. She is the *raconteur*, not the *vates ;* the scientist, not the seer.

RECIPROCITY

RECIPROCITY.

THE word reciprocity is used to denote the *quid pro quo* which inheres in all our relations with each other—the *give and take* of the common lot ; those mutualities which the mere fact of living makes our privilege and our duty ; the debit and credit of every-day affairs ; the roll of our liabilities and assessments as members of the great firm of humanity. Shakespeare said, "All the world's a stage, and men and women are the actors." And his paraphrase has in it a great deal of truth, if a great deal of poetry ; doubtless there is something of the actor in each one of us ; doubtless you and I occasionally drop the common gait and slip into a grandiose stage-walk ; doubtless we assume a *rôle* we were not born to, and play our little play upon occasions, and shall continue to do so until the final drop of the curtain. But I think that to say all the world is a market, and men and women are the buyers and the sellers, would have in it more of truth if less of poetry. Indeed, this is the strictest verity. All the world is a market, and it is a market all the time ; and all the men and women are buying and selling, and buying and selling all the time. The barter never ceases ; we are constantly offering something in exchange for something else, and constantly having like bargains pressed upon us. This is the situation ; into it we are born. It is not of our making, and cannot be of our unmaking. We are so related to each other that we are perforce giving and taking, and we cannot be otherwise.

It is the aspiration of many a soul to be self-sufficing. Independence is a butterfly we chase summer and winter, but we never catch it. Among all delusions by which we flatter ourselves in this market of life, I know of none more honest and more vain than this, that we are actually independent, that we depend only upon ourselves, that no one is necessary to us.

Perhaps not one of us is without a personal convincing experience of the impossibility of standing alone in this world. I suspect a brief experience is sufficient; it is one of which we are not proud, and which we are not eager to exhibit. In truth, it is ridiculous if not pathetic, this attempt to get along alone—ridiculous because so plainly to other eyes a failure; pathetic because to one's own eyes the ridiculousness is so invisible. Occasionally a conspicuous example illustrates our proposition. Witness beautiful, wayward Thoreau, astride of his preferred pumpkin in his wilderness, lord over no man, lorded over by none, and believing himself independent of heart, independent of head, as he was independent in all material affairs. Yet let his own charming confession, albeit unconscious, show us how his human heart unloaded itself of love to sylvan creatures. What perfect reciprocity of affection was between him and the squirrels, birds, fishes! How his large, involuntary lovingness depended on them for companionship! How that intellect which he deprived of converse with the living, yet held communion in that wilderness with the sages and seers of the past! How his mind depended on their intellectual *camaraderie*—none the less, to Thoreau, *camaraderie*, because wholly ghostly.

Many a one has had Thoreau's dream, few have come so near realizing it as he ; and he utterly failed of it. Aristotle said : " Whosoever is delighted in solitude is either a wild beast or a god.'' We have in us a good deal of each, but yet we are neither, and self alone could never suffice us. No ; independence, in an absolute sense, is an impossibility. The nature of things is against it. The human soul was not made to contain itself. It was made to spill over, and it does and will spill over, always as *quid pro quo*, wheresoever lodged, to the end of time. Reciprocity, constant and equal, among all His creatures is the plan of the only Maker of plans, whose plans never fail in the least jot or tittle. He has reserved to Himself the power to give without receiving. Everywhere, even among rudest nations, has this principle of reciprocity between man and man been recognized, and ideals of governments have been erected on it.

Yes, life is a market, and men and women are the marketers. There is no getting away from it. Young men and young women stand at the threshold of their career, and debate what shall be their calling. It is a matter of choice. They are free to select their pursuit or profession. But the circumscribing profession has already swept its line around them ; they are not free here. Into this or that vocation were they born, and the vocation they choose is included in this hereditary one. Some stand in the marketplace of life as preachers, some as teachers, some as physicians, some as jacks-of-all-trades, jobbers, old-maid aunts—whose profession is more imperious than any I know.

But however our services are sub-rented, each stands indentured to the law of the overload of life, the law of reciprocity. Consciously or unconsciously life is but one long *quid pro quo.*

> " We cannot live, except thus mutually
> We alternate, aware or unaware,
> The reflex act of life ; and when we bear
> Our virtue outward, most impulsively,
> Most full of invocation, and to be
> Most instantly compellent, certes, there
> We live most life, whoever breathes most air
> And counts his dying years by sun and sea !"

I.

A very large proportion of what we consciously or unconsciously offer in exchange is on the surface ; it is what we call manners. I beg you to consider what is the extent of the realm of manners ; how it covers the whole outside of us. It is what we present to the eye of the world. It is all from which any, save the very few who go beneath the surface with us, have to judge from. How constantly we are confessing this fact in our excuses for our friend, whose manners offend some one who knows him less intimately than we do ! We say, " Oh, you must not mind that ; he did not mean anything by it ; it is only his manner !" But all the same, this which we plead is only his manner has made its indelible impression. Your manner, your use or abuse of the forms of social life, the surface you offer, is the most extensive, if not the deepest, depart-

ment of your commercial transactions in this realm of commerce which we are considering. Your enemy as well as
your friend must deal with you here. The merest acquaintance makes some exchange with you. I cannot come
in from a walk on the village street without something more
or less than when I started out. Somebody has offered me
a smile, and I have given something back. A genuine
smile generally brings its price in a genuine smile back.
Somebody has saluted me respectfully, and that person is
paid in his own coin.

But the manners which I know I offer, the bows I can see
myself making, the attitudes I take, the greetings, the
forms of social deportment, the conversation, the acquired
and conscious reciprocity here, however important, sink
into insignificance beside the unconscious, the impossible
to acquire. And here we come to the gravest consideration of all ; here we strike upon the truth which con-
nects the department of surface manners with the deepest
depths and the highest heights. Conscious and acquired
manners we may, though not wisely, sneer at ; we may refer
them to the realm of the dancing-master and silly little gilt-
edged books on etiquette ; but the surface which is unconscious, and which cannot be acquired, and which, *nolens
volens*, we *must* present—that has nothing in common with
the Turveydrops. That belongs to the realm of the seers,
and the philosophers, and the theologians. For no study
of social forms can prevent the thoughts of the brain, the
intents of the heart striking through the surface. The real
grain will show beneath the varnish. This unconscious and
self-revealing give and take in the surface-life prevails
everywhere and always, even in books whose writers have

passed away. I do not suppose Dr. Johnson was aware that he was offering battle to his readers when he bargained with his bookseller. I suppose the conscious bargain between himself and his readers was that of wit, and wisdom, and learning in exchange for fame. But an unconscious *bonus* was thrown in. The great lexicographer's rudeness, his gratuitous insults, his grinding small and grinding all—in short, his manners, were an inseparable part of his wares and of himself, and his buyers return him dislike with their admiration. I do not suppose the young lady whom Lamb has immortalized as "Hester" was conscious of that historic smile of hers, so lavishly squandered in her morning salutation to the little essayist. She was unconscious that he got from

> . . . "her cheerful eyes a ray
> That struck a bliss upon the day,
> A bliss that would not go away."

And she got in return an immortality as long as Lamb's. It was simply a matter of manners on her part. Your manners and mine are not so much our own as they are somebody else's. Manners are made in the market where they are sold, and their buying and their selling are mostly unconscious. A man is known by the company he keeps. One must be Carlyle himself if he can keep Carlyle's manners, in constant company with Jane Welch, and the gentle spirits that scintillated around her. Observe how Dante's manners differ as he moves among the circles of the Inferno and the Paradiso, and how uniformly he was the poet to Virgil.

II.

Thoughts are a prime article of commerce. The intellectual life is everywhere that of reciprocity ; the products of the brain are articles of constant export and import. So true is this, so continual and confused is the barter, that we sometimes cannot tell if we bring a thought to or from the market ; the *meum* and *tuum* become involved.

But there can be no monopoly here. People sometimes say : " I have no goods in this line ; it is not my department of the market. You must go to the professional thinkers, to the teachers, and preachers, and bookmakers, and newspaper men.'' So the unprofessional thinkers keep their thoughts to themselves, and corners are created. And there is no nobler work that any one of you could set yourself to than to break up these intellectual corners. We must begin this worthy work by being honest. We must open our granaries, and offer our hoarded thoughts in exchange. There is a vast amount of thinking which ought to be in the market. We hold our best thoughts, and give our second best. It never occurs to us that we are dishonest in deal here. Or, if any one accuses us of a debt in this direction, we get off with one excuse or another, which seems to us sufficient and even creditable. How many of us excuse this second-best character of the thoughts we give to others in conversation by the plea that we are not original thinkers, that we have no original ideas ! A lame and impotent conclusion, and no excuse at all. Nothing is worse for you than to think yourself not an original person, except to think that you are an original person. Do not flatter yourself in either direc-

tion. You are as original as anybody else, and no more so.
There are no original people, in fact. Everybody thinks,
and everybody thinks about everything. Adam was the last
original thinker. It is not likely there have been any new
thoughts outside the Garden of Eden. That which wins
for the thinker the title of original is not the newness—
or *firstness*—of his thoughts ; but the newness, perhaps
firstness, of his expression of them in their relation to other
thoughts, their method and extent of elaboration. That this
is true is proven by the reception given the original thinkers, preachers, writers, teachers. At once they are called
original, and the fact that they are called so proves that
they are not so. It is because their thoughts are the very
thoughts of their hearers, readers, scholars, but so surpris-
ingly dressed up, come at by routes so unfamiliar, confronted so unexpectedly, elaborated to such distinctness.
It is not an introduction to a stranger, but the sudden
encounter with an old friend, altered, wonderfully improved, developed beyond our dreams, but still the one we
knew before. It is only because it is our very own that we
are so delighted, so thrilled. We call him original who
makes us original ; for he makes us discover ourselves to be
thinkers also. The transition from unconscious to conscious thought is education. Learning a thing truly is but
recognizing it. A scholar never knows his lesson until he
understands it, and understanding it is thinking it for himself. When he says at last of his problem, " I understand
it," he says, " That is my own thought." He confesses
that it would be a possibility for him to have written the
geometry.

It should be our serious business to become conscious

of our own thoughts ; to stand in the great intellectual marts
of life, aware that we have a right there, that all its treasures are free to us by reason of stock-ownership.

We can do no better work than to stimulate the utterance
of thought. Mrs. Browning's conversation, it is said, was
pre-eminently *tête-à-tête*. She was a most conscientious and
magnetic listener. She compelled reciprocity of thought.
Madame de Staël was great in talking, but George Eliot
was greater in making other people talk. I am con-
vinced that people think enough ; it is the utterance
of thought that is needed. If the habit of brave attempt
at this utterance could be formed, and, despite all criticism, be persevered in, how much more should we give to
each other ! What a world of enjoyment and improvement
would spring up ! How Athenian would Yankee life become ! A Socrates at every doorway, an Aspasia—without
Aspasia's reproach—at every tea-urn, full of discourse that
would exclude the weary pettiness of thoughtless talk. Do
this for your neighbors, and you will be to them Ferdinands
and Isabellas, making of them the discoverers of more than
a continent, for they will discover themselves ; and you will
pay to them the debt you owe to those who have done the
same for you. But do not conceive yourself an original
person. It is a snare and a delusion.

III.

It is not in the superficial reciprocities of social life,
in the realm of manners, in the exchange of courtesies and
forms—not in the commerce of intellectual life, in the

interchange of thought, that the law of reciprocity is most influential. It is in the affections that we make our best and worst bargains, our most saving and most ruinous exchanges.

In the fresh young years of our lives there is a facility of feeling, a readiness of devotion, a reckless expenditure of faith and love. We who have forever passed beyond those years of glorious prodigality may well expend a sigh upon their loss, and deem the calculating wisdom of our later lives a dubious exchange. Oh, those days of opulent bankruptcy, when we were rich in outlawed debts of friendship—those wealthy insolvencies, when we owed everybody, and everybody owed us, love, and faith, and loyalty ! How quickly did our broken banks begin again their reckless discount ! How promptly were our foreclosed mortgages of heart re-leased ! . . .

Are you suffering, and do you attribute your suffering to unreciprocated affection ? Your diagnosis is wrong. You are the victim again of a delusion. Less possible than absolute independence, than original thought, is unreciprocated affection. I do not undertake to convince you of this truth. I am content to state it, and leave its demonstration to the long run. I have unbounded faith in the long run. Sydney Smith said that in order to preserve contentment we must take short views of life. I think in order to preserve contentment we must take long views, very long ones. Your affection was not unrequited. Something came back for it, if it was genuine, and something that was *quid pro quo.* I never condole with the person of " blighted affections," because I know that to true affection no blight is possible. Its argosies are out at sea; they have not made their desired haven, but they will cruise around and come back with a Golden Fleece.

A flirt is the most harmless person in the world. A genuine flirtation is the fairest bargain possible—nothing for nothing, *nihil ex nihilo*. The battle is like that between Milton's Michael and Satan—if one gets hurt, he recovers immediately—for flirts are ethereal creatures; you can walk through them and not know there is anything there; like those Miltonic spirits, they

> " . . . can in all their liquid texture mortal wound
> Receive no more than can the fluid air."

It is all a matter of tenuous reciprocity.

Shall we speak of our bargains in love and friendship? Shall we venture to argue the question of reciprocity between us and our friends? Ah, how little patience we should have in the attempt! How well we are aware of the generous barter; how certain we are that we are the gainers; how assured that in every true friend we have the best of the bargain!

There is, indeed, no room for argument here. Love balances all accounts. In place of argument the story of Richard, lion-hearted, comes to me; of Richard languishing a captive, hidden from sight and sound of any comrade in an enemy's land; of Blondel, standing finally, after long and vain search, beneath that prison-window, and sending up to it, by way of experiment, one couplet from a song he and his royal friend had composed and sung together. Instantly the next verse comes floating from behind the

prison grating down to Blondel, and Richard is discovered
and regained.

Such is the reciprocity of hearts, so souls wander in
search of each other, so many a royal heart languishes in
exile, till beneath its prison-bars love stands and sings its
own familiar and enchanting song !

But now comes the practical consideration of our subject
in the questions which are its logical outcome. What is
our personal status in the market, what the ethics that regu-
late our reciprocal transactions ? Are we making good bargains ? Are we honest in deal ? Are we getting rich or
poor ? How is it in the department of manners ? Manners are not character, but they are the dress of character.
Character does not at once show for itself ; manners show
for it. How have we clothed our character ? Does its
dress do it justice ? Does it fitly present it to the eye ? If
not, then we are unfair in deal with a double dishonesty —
injustice to ourselves and injustice to others. Others invest in what they believe to be ourselves, according as our
manners present us to them ; and whether they are deceived
in their investment or not is our responsibility in the dress
we give our characters. Our manners may cheat other people to our advantage or our disadvantage. They should yield
us a good income. Manners are of the surface and of
the moment. They do not have to do with the depths and
the long run ; yet it is by the surface that we enter the
depths, and the moments make the long run.

For all that others, our teachers, our preachers, our authors,
have painfully forged out into shapely gold for our enrich-
ment, what are we returning ? What is our thought within
us, what is it without ? When a high thought comes, do

we fling it abroad with liberal soul, or do we fold it away in a napkin that becomes its grave-cloth ? If we do this latter, then we are dishonest in deal, for we owe that thought to the world. A great deal of this interment of our best thought-life is justified to ourselves by the plea that such thoughts are too sacred for utterance : a wretched sophistry, a miserable excuse for what is really our fear of criticism, our shamefacedness of spiritual life. There are some peo- ple who seem to be afraid of nothing so much as that they will cast their pearls before swine. I have observed that these people are not apt to be the best judges of either pearls or pork.

Ah me ! what does our tasteless babble need so much as the savor of high thought ? What do we need so much to see as that which is sacred ? Who of us cannot recall the magic transmutation that took place when, some time in the midst of idle talk, a brave soul threw down a golden thought amid all the clattering rubbish—some gleam from the life of the spirit, some sacred jewel of inner life ? How it hushed the chatter ! How grateful, if rebuked, we felt ! How encouraged ourselves to utter that which we had not dared to speak when all utterance was so different from it ! How much more this brave spirituality of our friend has helped us than any words that came to us from priest or from poet, from pulpit or from book ! We can do no braver or better thing than to bring our best thoughts to the every-day market. They will yield us usurious interest.

How is it in our friendships ? Have we given faith for faith, loyalty for loyalty, truth for truth ? Have our hearts sought out the needy ? Have we cast our bread upon the waters ? If ye love them that love you, what reward have

ye ? do not even the publicans the same ? Have we risen
above the plane of the publicans ?

These are among the most weighty questions we can ask
ourselves. But we can answer them only in part, for the
greater proportion of that which we carry, or, rather, which
goes with us to the world of social, intellectual, emotional,
and spiritual life, is unconscious. The greater part of that
which comes to us is unconscious. It makes part of us, but
we do not detect ourselves in receiving it. Our most important bargains never announce themselves. We have no
scales by which to measure these commodities of brain, and
heart, and spirit. We cannot apply the mathematics of the
money market here. We have no science for this book-
keeping that can compass all its complexity of exchanges,
follow the winding course of this commerce as it makes its
indirect returns, detect the subtle equities of this ceaseless,
silent reciprocity !

But, for all our inability, the books are kept. When the
long run has run out we shall confront exact balances, *quid
pro quo*, to the uttermost farthing.

I suppose that if you and I could know just what and all
were the elements of reciprocity between us, and all who
deal with us—just what was being exchanged between us,
what were our bargains, and who the parties to them, we
should be amazed, perhaps appalled. Well may we ask
with eagerness how the market is to-day ; how it goes on
'Change. For everything is at stake here ; our very all is
invested. It is only the golden rule, "Do unto others as ye
would that they should do unto you," which opens to us
the secret of fair deal, of good bargains, of wealth incalculable ! I congratulate you, whoever you be, if you can

square the conscious and yet more the unconscious transactions in the barter of your mental and spiritual life by the measurements of this rule. This is the chief thing, the *rule* within us. Goethe said, "It is the spirit in which we act which is the great thing." It is the *spirit* in which we traffic which is the great thing. It is, indeed, all.

We may well be thrilled when we remember how constant and how instant is the tide of reciprocity 'twixt one and all, 'twixt brain, and heart, and spirit of all who live, so that not one can say, "I am alone ; I am independent ; I am nothing to any one who lives, not one is anything to me." We may well exult when we realize the dignity it puts upon each one of us as members of this great human society ; the importance with which it clothes us, the responsibility with which it endows us, the riches to which it makes us heir !

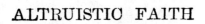

ALTRUISTIC FAITH

ALTRUISTIC FAITH.

Cadijah! What image does the name evoke? The
image, I venture, if any, of a very distinct and magnificent
face—of eyes dark yet glowing, like a midnight full of stars,
of flowing, silky beard, of turban folded over prophetic
locks—the face, not at all of Cadijah, but of Mahomet.
There is no biography of Cadijah, and no portrait. All
that we certainly know of her is that she was Mahomet's
first wife, a noble and wealthy widow, whom he wedded
when he was twenty-five and she much older, and to whom
he was singly devoted and faithful up to the time of her
death.

How, then, may this woman, standing in the darkness
which gathers around the vestibule of the Middle Ages,
offer from her poverty of resource anything worth our
while to consider, we

" The heirs of all the ages in the foremost files of time " ?

Years after the death of Cadijah, when Ayesha, the
beautiful girl, the pet child-wife of Mahomet's old age,
arrogant with the arrogance of a beauty and a favorite,
attempted to rally her now illustrious and powerful husband
upon his loyal love for his first wife, and said to him,
" Was she not old? and has not God given you a better
in her place?" Mahomet replied, with an effusion of hon-

est gratitude, " No, by Allah ! there can never be a better. She believed in me when men despised me."

" *She believed in me !*"   From Mahomet's own lips we have our question answered.   Cadijah offers to us a splendid and immortal example of the *effectual, fervent faith of one soul in another.*   And this it is of which I have to speak.   Not of the Mahomets, except by implication, but of Cadijah, whose faith has wrought out Mahomet, since ever the world began — whose faith must still evolve him so long as the world lasts and Mahomets survive.

Faith is a Trinity.   It is one—faith in God ; and it is three—faith in God, faith in self, and faith in humanity.   Faith in God is the unit, the integral designation of this Trinity, for it includes by logical necessity both the other faiths.   Whether men admit it or not, faith in ourselves and faith in our brother and sister humanity follow from our faith in God, and if that faith be allowed its full growth, will each win their rightful rank. But because our faith in God is so rarely allowed its full growth, these other faiths—faith in ourselves and faith in each other—do not come into full view and win due recognition.

We repeat our creed, " I believe in God, the Father," but we do not always realize that this creed includes, " I believe in myself," and " I believe in other people."   Yet this threefold faith should be taught.   A true belief in God is threesided, and the glory of the God-side was never meant to obscure the brightness of the other two sides, but rather to render them conspicuous.

It is of the most neglected of these minor faiths that I

wish to speak—the altruistic faith, or faith in other than self.

By the term, abstract altruistic faith, I mean to imply that general attitude of mind which is hopeful and expectant of humanity ; a faith in human nature's intrinsic worth and capability ; a faith which beholds man, as in Nebuchadnezzar's dream, sadly and mysteriously mixed of things precious and things base ; but which beholds as clearly the head of fine gold and the breast of silver as the feet of iron and clay ; a faith that the race is steadily gravitating toward a goal of final good rather than evil ; a faith that, when the averages of the ages are accurately struck, the leverage will be found to be constantly upward, not downward ; a faith that humanity is persistently electing itself to honor, glory, and immortality by a majority which secures to the same party all future canvasses ; a faith which wavers not an instant before the question, however cleverly put by the pessimist, " Is life worth living ?" but responds with an immediate and hearty, " Yes, a thousand times *Yes!* Life is infinitely worth living !" A faith which looks into poorhouses, and idiot asylums, and penitentiaries —ay, and into the darkness of great cities by night, and still believes in humanity reclaimable, however marred or fallen, and infinitely worth saving. A faith which contemplates the catastrophe of moral obliquity and spiritual suicide ; of the mole and the bat-life of thousands of us ; of the leprous spawn of human beings that are constantly thrown upon the shores of life only to contaminate and curse, and yet which says, with Longfellow,

> " I believe that in all ages
> Every human heart is human ;

> That in even savage bosoms
> There are longings, yearnings, strivings,
> For the good they comprehend not ;
> That the feeble hands and helpless,
> Groping blindly in the darkness,
> Reach God's right hand in that darkness,
> And are lifted up and strengthened."

But the abstract faith is subordinate—an effect rather than a cause. For generalities and abstractions do not demand our prolonged consideration. Our lives are not laid out in vast, vague prairies, but in definite domestic door-yards, within which we are to exercise and develop our faculties. Altruistic faith in the abstract is most valuable, but it is, at best, but a passive rather than an active possession. We cannot touch humanity at large except as we touch humanity in the individual. Altruistic faith must exercise itself upon concretions, not abstractions, if it be a real power for good. One may possess a whole Milky Way of vague general belief in humanity, and yet it may be of less avail to the benighted traveller than a single rushlight put sympathetically into his hand. We must focus our faith upon the individual in order to get or to give the good of it.

This concrete altruistic faith does not require for its exercise that its possessor belong to the female sex. The contrary idea is, I fear, deeply rooted in the public mind. There is a very general impression that it is in the *nature of things* that woman should walk principally by faith, and that this faith should be principally altruistic. I myself confess to a lurking suspicion that it is oftener a woman than a man who is a Cadijah. It may be easier for a woman to believe in somebody else than for a man to do so. Men, as a rule, are very much occupied with believing in themselves. Woman is confessedly altruistic, but not exclusively so. Carlyle had his Cadijah in his wife ; George Eliot had hers in her husband.

But this faith, though not inconsistent with the estate of holy matrimony, is yet not dependent upon that estate. I use the name Cadijah to represent the character of an efficient believer in somebody else ; but Cadijah could have exercised her faith in Mahomet to its full effect on his fortunes without having been his wife. The exercise of Mrs. Carlyle's faith in her husband had nothing to do with the exercise of her hands and feet upon the Craigenputtock kitchen-floor. Cadijah may or may not have a passionate personal love for her Mahomet, but she will not be so " in love" with him as to induce the blindness of that undesirable condition. Pascal said : " In order to know God we must love Him ; in order to love man we must know him." I am not sure that all love for individual man depends upon knowing him ; there is love and love, but the rational, lasting love must admit, at least, if not demand, for its persistence, some real acquaintanceship. To all love that rightly culminates in marriage there is, doubtless, an irrational phase, a normal abnormality that may or may not outlast the honeymoon, and then gives place to something better. In this period no Cadijah can flourish ; indeed, the conditions of concrete altruistic faith do not demand the conditions of courtship or of marriage. Cadijah-ism is not necessarily connubiality.

Nor is this faith hero-worship. We all have our heroes who are veritable heroes to us, frequently for no other reason than because we cannot be *valets* to them. And that

is well and good. But the one to whom you are Cadijah
will not be a hero to you. You will serve him, but you
will not worship him. Cadijah never imagines, as do the
worshippers, that her Mahomet can do or be anything he
may please, or she may please. She perceives that he can
do and be *one* thing, and possibly that this is the thing
which pleases him not. She does not discover him to be a
predestined prophet or a born poet because her love or ambition elect him to be such. It may be, rather, that her faith
discerns in him supreme capabilities for a dry-goods clerk or
a ranchman. No. Though my Cadijah love me as her own
soul, and have set her whole heart on me, she cannot, this
clear-eyed Cadijah of mine, persuade herself that I can
be what I cannot be. She can only perceive me to be
what I *can* be. Cadijah is a seer, but she is not a vision-
ary. She wields a diviner's rod, but not a wizard's wand.
The historical Cadijah was, I venture, greatly enamored of
her young and handsome lord. But I am not sure she
thought him a great prophet or a spotless priest. What
I *am* sure of is, that this shrewd, devoted woman perceived
him to be a born predestined leader, a man of destiny, one
to sway multitudes with the mighty magnetism of his personality ; a man to beckon and be followed ; a man to
speak and be believed ; a man to command and be obeyed.
She saw the oak in the acorn with this sixth sense of hers.
She believed in him when all men despised him, but she did
not give him hero-worship.

It is clear that to Mrs. Carlyle her husband was not a
hero. As an apostle of silence and several other things he
was a great joke to her. But as a man of ideas, great, gro-
tesque, forceful, propulsive, full of the vitality of immortal

genius, worthy and destined to live in literature, as such she
saw him when his fame was yet in embryo. And this faith
of hers in his power to do never flagged until it became
sight before all the world, a wisdom justified of her children. And this is not hero-worship. It is a far finer and
usefuler thing.

To speak affirmatively, this quality of the Cadijahs I define as that faculty in my friend by which he discriminates in
me what I am good for—nay, what I am *best* for. That one
who comes to me, resolute for me when I stand irresolute
for myself, at that point in my straight turnpike where by-
roads fork out from it—that one who comes to me while I
waver in view of the old highway and cast lingering glances
at the new byways, and who, with hand uplifted and with
finger pointed straight before, says to me, with emphasis of
unalterable conviction, " This is *your* way ; this, no other,
the path which leads you to your goal !" this man, or this
woman, is my Cadijah. He may or may not have vehement
love for me, but if he has vehement faith in me, and gives
me the benefit of its momentum, he is my friend, and
" there can never be a better," for he believes in me when
a worse than the despising of men has befallen me—the
despising of myself ! " *Quand tout est perdu, c'est le
moment des grandes âmes,*" said Lacordaire. A grand soul
is Cadijah ; she comes to me when all is lost ! How common to us all is the experience of meeting one who seems
to have a peculiar insight into our character, so that we say,
" He *divined* me." How often do we hear it said, " He
seems to understand me better than any one else. " " She
appreciates me more truly than any one ever has." This
quality of *divination* is the intellectual element of altru·

istic faith. It is not the whole of it, for another element lies in the will and is essential ; but it is the extraordinary element, and far from infrequent.

The one is gift, the other grace. The one prerogative, the other duty. It is always true that the thing that ought to be done is the thing that can be done. It is not always true that the thing that can be done is the thing that *ought* to be done. But in the exercise of altruistic faith there is certainly and always an *ought* where there is a *can*, and a *can* where there is an *ought*. When the intellect says, " I can," the heart should say, *I will*.

Each of us can so believe in humanity in general as to contribute to that pressure which constantly levers up the race ; can surround ourselves with an atmosphere optimistic rather than the contrary ; can believe in some one or more individuals so as to be the determining factor in their careers, as was Cadijah in the career of Mahomet, as was Jane Welch in the career of Carlyle.

I never knew a good man or a good woman who was not practically an optimist. I have personally known several, impersonally many, who were not nominally optimists, but wholly the contrary ; they did not know themselves as such, but other people did. It was simply a misunderstanding as to the name. I have in mind a woman of great influence, whose sphere circumscribes many important individuals, and whose whole life is encouraging and helpful ; whose whole burden of exhortation to each and all is, to make the best of it, because there is a best to be made ; to try over and over, because it is always worth while ; and why worth while, except that success is possible, and if possible, certain to the indomitable ? This woman has been a Cadijah to more than one individual ; has hindered suicide, and out of a perverse profound of obliquity in one life brought obedient order and uprightness by her simple conviction that it *ought* to be so ; to another she has been a stimulus to faith in his own genius and to continued effort, simply because of her faith in that genius, her faith in the capacity for that effort ; and yet the tortures of the Inquisition would not wring from this woman a *credo :* to every assertion that the race is better living than dead ; that it is, on the whole, constantly gaining toward the goal ; that human nature progresses rather than retrogrades, and that, after all, human life is, in a general and particular sense, *worth while*—to all such statements she but wistfully shakes her head, and wishes it were so. She is living, and may die under the impression that she is a pessimist. Yet this woman has more altruistic faith, in the abstract even, than almost any one I know. In short, one who has that faith in the concrete is sure to have it in the abstract ; and the effect is that of optimism in the world. If Byron had had sufficient altruistic faith in some one (and that one not a beautiful woman !) to make that person's life worth living, he would never have so lost all conscience concerning his influence as to have written :

> " Count o'er the joys that thou hast seen,
> Count o'er the hours from anguish free,
> And know, whatever thou hast been,
> 'Twere something better not to be !"

The surest way to get the wider altruism is to exercise the special altruism. No one whose faith in another was such as to determine the career of that other ever halted there ; such an one must believe in the race.

And this brings me back to the core and pith of my mat-

ter.   I exhort you to the exercise of altruistic faith in the
concrete.   I say to you, Believe in somebody—somebody in
particular.   An abstract altruism is good ; but if it ripens
not into the concrete there is something wrong.   One of
my friends has a character in one of her plays who " does
nothing else but lie awake nights and rock days, thinkin'
how she can be doing good."   Her altruism is too abstract.
That one who says truly :

> " I live for those who love me,
>   For those who know me true,
>   For the heaven that smiles above me,
>   And the good that I can do,"

never fails to so specialize this altruism as to be the making
of more than one individual man.   Do not concern yourself
first about the race ; do not expend much time or thought
on introspection as to whether you believe life to be worth
living.   I venture to say that if the author of that remarkable book, "Is Life Worth Living?" had occupied himself in making life worth living to one or more of his fellow-
men, not in the general way of well-wishing and money-
giving, but in the particular way of discovering to some
hopeless man the special aptitude in him, the painstaking
way of recognizing as good for something, and good for
something in particular, some individual or individuals who
felt themselves good for nothing—I venture to say that if
he had so occupied himself—so attitudinized his mind—he
would have found no time for the pessimistic studies and
analyses with which he treats the momentous question.

For the question is momentous.   In asking it we ask
every other question which concerns the race or the individual.   But it concerns the individual first, the race last.

It may well affright—nay, appall us, as we look within our lives for an answer, desperately desiring to find material for an affirmative. Let this inward look be very brief, but let it be very thorough. Let us descend into the depths of all that inalienable experience which has gone into the making of our lives. God pity us in that groping, unless here and there glimmers a taper of altruism to light up the abyss of selfishness ! Out of the blackness of this darkness we shall emerge to objective realities forever color-blind to any brightness for the race, or for self, unless we can bring up hither that torch of faith in *other than self*.

We shall find life so worthless that we would not care for its continuance unless we have made, are making, or shall make somebody else's life worth living, which other life, except for us, had not been, in the end, so worth while.

That last is, after all, the saving clause—"*except for us !*" It fortifies us against disbelief in ourselves. We must each feel that what we do another could not do ; else, after all, our existence is not necessary, and, in the last analysis, who cares to live an unnecessary life—a life that could be dispensed with—and the result remain the same ? No, the noble soul would choose rather not to be than not to be somebody in particular. Herein consists that which so much fascinates and so much misleads in the dogmas of Buddhism. The Eastern mystic realizes that man's life, as men live it, being filled with selfish passion, is not worth living—cannot be in the nature of things. It is vain to try to make it so. The individual will never subordinate selfish passion to altruistic faith—passion will subtly work for self, and surely undo any strivings of the faith for others— it is time wasted to attempt to make the *ego* good for something ; it is good for nothing, good only to lose ! One cannot be—was not meant to be (since he cannot be)—anybody in particular ; therefore the *summum bonum* is to lose the one in the all, which is Nirvâna. He does not even dwell upon the possibility of a nobler alternative. It is inconceivable that this full-blooded *ego*, living his intense individual life, can ever, save as the dupe of demon deceivers, who pervert perception and destroy reflection, have a conscious thrill of exultation in his individual life, because he knows that there has good come to the race which, except for his individual life, would not have come. No, no ; the only best is to lose the *ego*, the only bliss is the luxury of its nullification.

The Eastern mystic does well on his plane. His choice is noble since he has no more to choose from ; he admits no better than his best. But his plane is below the highest ; he dwells upon the stair, and forever just misses the landing !

Many more than the Eastern mystic move on this plane, dwell on this stair, and miss the landing. But our Western Buddhist cannot be so joyous in his pessimism, because he cannot be so selfish. He belongs to the breeze-impelled, forward-moving race of the restless, pushing genius, the genius which admits no condition good enough to be let alone. This Western thinker knows that the intensest individual life is the highest duty of the man created in God's image ; that the supremest living is to fully bring out that image of the Father in the child, in the farthest development and finest finish of that child, separate and distinct from all other individuals of the human family ; and he feels the pain of this responsibility, which no one can lift from him—this responsibility of the development and finish of this *ego;* that *ego* whom he can never hide from final Omnipotent scrutiny and sentence. And he knows, because of his fatal certainty here, that he cannot innocently give the Eastern mystic his company. He knows that the Eastern mystic's highest would be his very lowest. He knows his life can be worth living, that therefore he can never be blameless in losing it. He knows that whatever it may consciously be to the Brahmin, to him it must consciously be the most hideous and gigantic selfishness to put all things behind him, except the extinction of self ; to sit cross-legged under a palm-tree extinguishing the *ego*—*i.e.*, throwing off all responsibilities to others, in order to attain the eternal irresponsibility.

No ; we of the West writhe and wince under the truth ; we would willingly shirk it, but we cannot. Each of us is born to be somebody in particular to himself or herself, and to others. This is the only solution of our being at all ; and if it does not answer the question, Is life worth living ? then there is no answer.

Let us enlarge and ennoble our capacity of altruistic faith—the capacity to be, in some life or lives, a Cadijah. There are those waiting for us to be this to them—for *us*, for you, for me, not another. There are those waiting for our recognition before men shall recognize them—nay, before they shall recognize themselves. From our lips their rightful name must fall, if it ever be heard.

No gift can pass between human creatures so divine as this gift of recognition, for it touches upon the creative. There is a sense in which it is true of some things that *saying so makes it so!* There are capabilities in each of us of which we are only half aware—capabilities that we never dare call by name, of which we need another's recognition before we fully admit their existence.

Of the most noble is this most true. Those in whom is most to recognize have most need of recognition. But not one lives who has not need of it. It may be your high privilege to recognize thus some artist, poet, painter. It may be yours to call such an one by his own true name before he can pronounce it for himself ; to pour baptismal oil upon him before the great ones have sent his fame forth and the spaniel herd that lick the footsteps of the leaders have caught it up. It may be yours to be Cadijah to a Mahomet, Jane Welch to a Carlyle, George Henry Lewes to a Marian Evans. If so, you are to be congratulated ; you may rightfully exult and say to the applauding, ratifying world, " I told you so !" It is your meed, your merit, your enduring fame. But it is not probable that to you and me, my friend, this lot, this meed, this merit, this enduring fame will fall. Not the less by jot or tittle are you and I to exercise the altruistic faith, and to exercise it concretely. The Mahomets, the Carlyles, the George Eliots, need their Cadijahs, but not so much, I would say—if comparison could be admitted here—as do the people with whom we come in contact every day, in common ways and common places. The perceptions of a Cadijah are not more needed to detect genius than to detect aptitude. It is mournful—nay, more, it is maddening—to observe how many people are misplaced in the highways and byways of life. Yet surely it is not more maddening to see a Charles Lamb blundering over accounts at a clerk's desk than to see Mr. John Smith, who should be there, writing essays in an attic. It is as truly the function of a Cadijah to say, You are *not*, as to say, You *are*.

To-day I met a woman who has discovered an aptitude for exquisite dress-making in a drudging shop-girl. The shop-girl has been simply a "hand," and this clever and good woman proposes to put this discovery of hers behind a brown-stone front, and fling out for her her true name in the magic *Mlle.* and *Modes*, which transform a sempstress into an artist. This woman does precisely the thing for the shop-girl which Cadijah did for Mahomet : she believes in her when other people do not. It is as legitimate an exercise of concrete altruistic faith to elect John Smith out of the essayist's attic into the counting-room as to take Charles Lamb out of the counting-room to Elia's library.

The best I can wish my readers is the blessing of a Cadijah in their lives. Much pitiful need and much painful want must mingle its bitter with the sweet of our experience before the full tale of our pilgrimage be told. Some of us, out of the weary suffering or distracting impotence of invalidism, will desperately crave the boon of health, and deem all else a glad exchange for it ; some of us, from the cramping limitations of poverty, will long sadly for the wealth that stands to us for opportunity and development ; and some of us, with health and wealth, will sicken with the loneliness that comes for the loss or lack of love, the passionate heart-craving which would gladly barter health and wealth in exchange for

" . . . the touch of a vanished hand
And the sound of a voice that is still."

Some one or all of these cravings will be ours. But I deem

it true that deeper than the craving for health, or wealth,
or love, is the craving for recognition, the deep desire to be
known for what we truly are ; to hear from some human lips
our rightful name—poet, preacher, painter, clerk, dress-
maker—whatever, by testimony of the conscious power
within us, we feel ourselves most fit for ; to *hear* this
name, that at last we may answer to it, and find and keep
our undisputed place. This desire, this need, is, I think,
the one beyond all others. If you miss health, miss wealth,
lose or lack love, may you *not* miss the gift from another
of divining faith in you ; this faith which is, as is all
faith, the gift of God. The name of every Cadijah is also
Theodora.

HISTORY

HISTORY.

I.

History is not an exact science. It cannot be reduced to formulas and equations and chronological tables. Yet this is the notion which many of us hold concerning it, and when we have learned lists of events and names, and are glib in chronology, we feel that we have studied history. Yet we have not studied history one whit more than the child, who has mastered the multiplication table, has studied music. Mathematics has to do with music, but mathematics is not music. Chronicle and chronology have to do with history, but they are not history. We must learn of the event; it is indispensable, but it is not the whole. We must take the event as a starting-point, and travel from it to the man and men behind it. We must obtain its accessories of time, and place, and circumstance; we must clothe the deed with the thought of which it is simply the skeleton; we must invest the career with the character, which is its spiritual body, without which it has no significance—in short, we must make of history simply what it is—a drama in which man, in multitudinous men, is the actor, whose time is all time, whose place is the past.

The past! What is the past? Is it naught to us but a cemetery wherein lie the perished men and women of the centuries behind ? Nay, far otherwise is the truth. There is a mediator between us and the past whose one hand we must hold as we tread these silent corridors ; that common spirit of humanity, living, potential, electric, which hovers amid the tablets and vitalizes all the dust.

It is this truth which we must possess, or, rather, of which we must be possessed, when we approach the realm of history. We must be saturated with a sense of kinship. A proper embarkation upon the sea of times past is a veritable voyage of discovery, and we should have in it the feelings which a fortune-hunter has who turns yellow parchments in search of proof of his relationship to the rich man who has died. For the past is simply humanity ; it is thou and I, a vast congregation of thous and I's : forest succeeding forest, sprout, sapling, tree, all the same multi form *ego* over and over to the end of time. Herein is the significance of the saying that history repeats itself. It does repeat itself, because it repeats its factors—the men and women who compose it. These factors are everybody. Adam stands at one end of the row, you and I at the other ; and, as in the children's game, we must "all take hold of hands." The spirit of a common humanity stands in the centre and gently re-unites wherever the ring is broken. Woe to us if we break rank. We are no longer in the game.

It is, therefore, this sympathy with the past which can unlock the inner halls of history and reveal to us its grandeur. Destitute of this, we are ever outside. We can get date, and name, and event, but we can never get at the company ; these things are but the furniture of the feast ; by them we make no acquaintance with the guests.

It is as if one walked in the forest with eyes upon the ground, picking up the fallen leaves of last year's summer. Such an one has in his possession but the herbarium of the past. He has walked in the forest and picked up the fallen leaves of date, and event, and career, and laid them away in the pages of his memory. This is the chronicler, and this is much. It is very good to have a herbarium. Far grander is it, I think, to walk in the forest with eyes to the green foliage overhead, cognizant of the life which animates all; penetrated with its bounty as it thrills the silences and winds up the arteries of the huge veterans of the woods; feeling the mould beneath trembling with the common life-blood. This is the historian. He, too, has a herbarium, but to his herbarium he carries a chemistry which restores to life each fallen leaf and hangs it in its proper place, juicy, verdant with perennial resurrection. He who has but the events of history has simply apprehension—knowledge, not that sympathetic comprehension which is wisdom. It is our privilege and our duty to carry this sympathy with us as we chronicle the event, and by its chemistry to win from the barren event the fruitful, vital idea of which it is but the chrysalis, to penetrate the integument career, and in its shining folds to find the character—the man. Thus do we make true acquaintance with those notable personages who shine down from the firmament of the times that have gone over us, as luminous nuclei toward which all eyes are drawn, raying illimitably their piercing light to the succeeding generations. Thus do we enter into the past and begin the study of history. Carlyle says : "Universal history, the history of what man has accomplished in this world, is, at bottom, the history of the great men who have worked here. They were the leaders of men, these great ones ; the modellers, patterns, and, in a wide sense, creators of whatsoever the general mass of men contrived to do or attain ; all things that we see standing accomplished in the world are properly the outer material result, the practical realization and embodiment of thoughts that dwelt in the great men sent into the world ; the soul of the world's history, it may justly be considered, was the history of these.''

Away, then, with that dwarfing notion of history which makes it mere record of events, and give its place to this true notion which makes it the drama of humanity. Let us cease to look in its pages for date and event ; let us commence to look therein for the formative ideas of the ages, and for the holders of these ideas, the man behind the thought, the makers of history. Let us study career as means only to the end—character. Let us realize that history is the shrine of humanity, humanity essential in its essence in past, present, future, wherein is stored the *ego*— the thou and the I.

We have now lost a wrong and acquired a right notion of the true character of history—a right notion which raises it to the level of psychology—a discourse concerning the soul of man ; and this is a truth, but not the whole truth. Another notion must be added which shall raise it to the altitude of a theology—a discourse concerning God, for this it surely is.

> "The undevout astronomer is mad."

He who perceives, as did Auguste Comte, that " the heavens declare no other glory than that of Hipparchus, of

Kepler, of Newton, and of all those who aided in establishing their laws''—he who gazes on the midnight heavens, who beholds the order of their march with its marvel and its mystery, and who interprets not their hieroglyph upon the scrolls of space into the plain handwriting of divinity —who, in the music of the spheres, discerns not that the theme of this celestial opera, in infinite refrain, is *God*, GOD, GOD ! he, indeed, is mad !

Less sane is he who reads the page of history, yet finds not between all lines the same great word ; who, seeing on the walls of all human institutions the flaming out of *mene* here, and *tekel* there, yet sees not the writer behind these walls ; who perceives how constant and instant is the conjunction in world-history of the hour and the man, yet sees not the unsleeping Watcher, who at the hour produces the man : this indeed is dulness of vision, dimness of eye, hardness of heart ! To one who acknowledges the man Christ to be the one top-flower of time, the perfect bloom of His life to be the final development of all that good toward which the heart of man in all ages has yearned—all history is sacred, and becomes, as it did to St. Augustine, but the history of the city of God, or to Jonathan Edwards, a " history of redemption," and all the past is but a panorama of Providence. Let a man believe in God, and he will find Him in history. I do not say he will find Calvinism there, as did Edwards, or any other *ism*. That he must first import into it before he can export it from it. To the agnostic, doubtless, history is but one long Walpurgis night of the past, from beginning to end ; he sees but a witch dance round a caldron from which no constant form emerges, but ever and anon, within its boil and

bubble, arises to evanescent view a momentary seeming,
which he christens destiny, or chance, or the unknowable.
But let the believer in God, the Father, gaze herein, and he
will see, as in the laboratory of some chemist, that all the
past is but the crucible of God ; he will perceive the creature God has made in successive transmutations, passed and
repassed in the fires of the ages ; and he will discern the
divine Alchemist bending over His creation with constant
patience and with perfect plan. Such an one will come
away from the pages of history rhythmic with the providence of God, with strengthened faith in both the Planner
and the plan ; he will see how, although

> " The old order changeth and yieldeth place to new,"

yet

> " God fulfils Himself in many ways."

Those who, with Longfellow,

> " . . . Believe that in all ages
> Every human heart is human,"

will find everywhere in history the conjunction of the
divine with this human ; will see how

> " In even savage bosoms
> There are longings, yearnings, striving
> For the good they comprehend not ;
> That the feeble hands and helpless,
> Groping blindly in the darkness,
> Clasp God's right hand in that darkness,
> And are lifted up and strengthened."

II.

How shall we study history?

In order to so study history that we shall get from it the most that can be gotten, I think three qualities are indispensable : conscience ; imagination ; industry.

Workmen and master ! Industry is the hand which, with unflagging patience, chips from those conglomerates called histories the petrified fact. Imagination is the re-creative breath which, falling close and ardent upon this fossil fact, restores to it life, and gathers back from out the past its whole environment ; and conscience is the righteous regulator and critic of the work of both.

Industry is essential. He who would penetrate into the complex facts of history in order that he may, in turn, be penetrated with the indivisible and universal truth of history, must not flinch before work. Morning by morning must he go forth to his toil ; and if in the evening he bring home little spoil, yet must he not complain. Much of his day must be spent in the rejection of the spurious ores which fall beneath his hammer, for not until he has laboriously excavated them, holding them off apart for careful scrutiny and comparison with the real, will he detect their falsity. Count, for instance, if you can, the counterfeit Napoleon Bonapartes you have rung upon the counter under the eye of conscience, before the true one, or its approximation, could be passed. Much of his day must be spent in divesting the true ore of alien substances. Tradition, myth, prejudice, so involve themselves with facts in history, that only patientest industry can set the facts clear. What an accumulation must first be stripped away from the story of Charlemagne, for instance, before the even approximately true historic figure can be seen ! Yet let not the industrious workman dream that his time so spent is wasted. It is his apprenticeship, and must be served. Facts of history must be gathered from history books, and from historic places, from everywhere, for the psychologist finds everywhere a harvest ; but industry alone is the harvester. Whether Lord Macaulay had genius or not may be questioned ; but that he had a thing as rare—industry—cannot be questioned. No journey was so long or difficult but he would take it, so he might the better satisfy himself concerning a fact of history. He must go to the spot and gather testimony there. Carlyle never made his " French Revolution," instinct with genius as it is, except by stupendous and indefatigable industry. He was fifteen years writing his " Frederick the Great." Hallam's " Middle Ages" has not a particle of the magnetism of genius in it, but will nevertheless stand to all time as a pre-eminently valuable historical work. Facts, and the getting of them—" *hoc opus, hic labor est !*"

Next comes imagination. Given the facts, and a properly trained imagination can evolve from them the truth. But the facts must be given. Imagination can do much, but she must have something to do with. She cannot create.

I use the word imagination in what I conceive to be its literal sense—image-making. It is a portrait painter by profession—nothing less, nothing more. And it paints fact-pictures and fancy-pictures. The first is its sphere in history ; both are its sphere in poetry.

When, as in Carlyle's " Cromwell," it assembles together
upon the foreground men and women who lived in the
past, objective realities, veritable flesh and blood humanity ;
when it puts acts and facts from the lives of these upon its
canvas, with actor, and time, and place, and scene, so that
we see the past as present, then it deals with the facts of
history, and the painter, however much a poet he may be,
has made a history.   When, as in " Paradise Lost," with
basis of fact and knowledge it makes the conceptions of the
brain objective realities, and depicts upon its canvas a man
who was never flesh and blood, a woman, alas ! never flesh
and blood, angels and devils, Satan and God, times, places,
scenes—all the fabric of a vision, why, then, imagination
deals with purely mental conceptions, and the painter,
however much a historian, has made poetry—or verse.

Now, both these are legitimate uses of the imagination,
with this difference, that while the maker of poetry may
have his choice of material, facts to which he may add
fancy *ad libitum*, or fancy *pur et simple*, the historian
must confine the exercise of his imagination most rigorously
to the bare facts of history.   And here he has need of his
stern task-master, conscience.   Given a fact in history, then
let imagination take this fact back to its time and place,
and there drape it with circumstance, and condition, and
atmosphere—in short, let it fly, with this captured fact,
back all the years that lie between to where the deed was
doing, the thought thinking, so that the personage whom
thought and deed preserve can be confronted in living presence ; a faculty this which treads closest of all upon the
God-like, since it can say to the dead, *Live again !*

This faculty is given us for use, and its use in the study

of history is to dramatize the past. But skill in its use is
not given ; that must be gained. It is something to be
learned, practised, perfected. It is, in brief, an art.

Industry is a simple thing. It is simply a sticking to, a
keeping on. There is no art about that. No one can
plead inability here. To keep on doing a thing you must
just keep on doing it. That is industry. But how properly to exercise the imagination that it may acquire power
to give you all the aid and just the aid you need in the
acquisition of history, that is not a simple thing. And
here we may learn from the masters.

Macaulay, with indefatigable industry, gave to his imagination all the material he could collect from books
and people ; and when his mind was so saturated with
the facts of his subject that he could no longer hold
them, he went to the place where the hero of his histories lived, or where the deed was done, and there gave
himself up to imagining the thing. And that is the way
he made his masterpieces historical paintings. What one
of our histories teaches us so much truth concerning that
remarkable personage, Julius Cæsar, as does the tragedy of
Shakespeare ? And how was this great work made except
by this same saturation of imagination ? The poet Campbell
says of this : " He" (the author of " Julius Cæsar ") " cast
his eyes, both in their quiet and in their kindled inspiration"
(*i.e.*, the eye, I take it, of industry and the eye of imagination), " both as poet and as philosopher, upon the page of
classic history ; he discriminated its characters with the
light of philosophy, and he irradiated *truth*, without en-
croaching on its solid shapes, with the hues of fancy. What
is Brutus but the veritable Brutus of Plutarch . . . un-

altered but hallowed to the imagination? What else is
Portia?"

Grace Greenwood writes from Belgium : " . . . An old
guide, who at the time of the battle of Waterloo was sev-
enteen years old, told us that he first conducted Victor Hugo
over the field. He said that the novelist stayed at a farm-
house in this neighborhood for two months, and walked
again and again over the ground of his marvellously vivid
scenes. That is the way an artist works!"

Yes, we say, "the way an artist works." The way a
Macaulay and a Hugo work. But we are not artists, not
Macaulays and Hugos, and we cannot work their way.

Yet here I think we make a great mistake. We do a
great deal of shirking in this life on the ground of not
being geniuses. The truth is, there is an immense amount
of humbug lurking in the folds of these specious theories
about genius. The exact quantum of genius in the world
is not ascertained any more than its exact definition. But
let a man or a woman go to work at a thing, and the genius
will take care of itself. It is not our business to look at
the masters in the light of geniuses, but only in the light of
workers. It is their duty to teach us, and ours to learn,
the best methods of work. Though we may never write
historical drama, or never paint with words a Waterloo, we
may go to work as did Macaulay and Hugo, and get what
history we do get as they got theirs. We may, with
patient and unflagging industry, accumulate our facts ; we
may live among them until our thought is saturated with
them, and then, pushing aside other things, call in Imagination and let her dramatize them to our vision. She will
stir them into vivid life, and the skeletons of the past will

assume face, voice, time, and place, and become men and women in the present.

"Too much trouble!" do we say?

Well, it is a good deal of trouble, I own, and *chacun à son goût.* I, for my part, would rather so realize one total character of history--as Queen Elizabeth—setting that mighty personage in dramatic action upon my mind's arena, by means of patient accumulation of the facts of her life, from babyhood to queenhood, studying her speeches, her manners, her tastes, her costumes, her associates, her favorites, her whole environment, until from the complete career the unit character was evolved, than to have all the histories of the realm of England, in complete chronological detail, at my tongue's end. I consider that far more would come to me in the former than in the latter case. An acorn in the mind is worth more than an oak forest at the end of the tongue. Taine says : " Genuine history is brought into existence only when the historian begins to unravel across the lapse of time the living man, toiling, impassioned, intrenched in his customs, with his voice and features, his gestures and his dress, distinct and complete as he from whom we have just parted in the street." And again : " I would give fifty volumes of charters and a hundred volumes of State papers for the memoirs of Cellini, the Epistles of St. Paul, the table-talk of Luther, or the comedies of Aristophanes."

Industry and Imagination ! Of these we have spoken, showing feebly how indispensable are both ; how easy the use of the former, how easy the misuse of the latter ; how both may be joined so that they shall together be made the engine of vast results. And in doing so we have left easy of inference all that need be said concerning Conscience, the vigorous task-master which we placed over the two work-men.

For who will persevere in industry unless Conscience stands by with uplifted lash ? One will work so long as enthusiasm keeps the purpose fresh, the motive bright. But when results are meagre and disappointments many— when the thing you hoped to hold as concrete fact glides off at last into a glittering generality, that most dangerous fiction—when the half truth in histories is so much mixed with the half lie, "ever the worst of lies"—when the authors of histories so differ that all must be examined to make any valuable—when philology is so loose and state-ment so careless—when event is so far in the past that much clutch upon it seems almost hopeless, why, then, enthusiasm wilts away, and if conscience be not near to keep us to our task, we will not be kept.

And if conscience be needful to keep industry up, it is still more so to keep imagination down. At this we have already hinted. It is a difficult thing to tell a story just as it happened, and yet make the story good. To be dramatic and at the same time accurate is a rare combina-tion. If the one is gift, the other is grace.

And here we come upon a great rock casting a portentous shadow. I know of but one besetment so easy in the study of history as that of credulity ; it is that of incredulity. If the one be Charybdis, the other is Scylla. Everywhere as we read we repeat the question we used to put so anxiously to the story-teller of our childhood, " Is this a true story ?" We read each one's account in order to try to find the fact, and the comment on all things, which Dickens makes his

dying miner utter to the woman he loved in vain, comes
back, "It's aw' a muddle, Rachel! It's aw' a muddle!"
When the friends of Horace Walpole sought to entertain
him on his death-bed by offering to read to him from
histories, he would reply, "Yes, bring me my liar!"
Incredulity besets us everywhere in our reading, and with
it comes the paralyzing "*cui bono?*"   And it is a chance
if our conscience be sufficient for either industry or imagination here.

The passage is indeed narrow, with Charybdis luring on
one side, and Scylla frowning on the other; yet there is a
way out. Our psychology must save us here. The *ego*
must steer us through. Do I wish to make acquaintance
with Napoleon Bonaparte, the "man of destiny," I must
accept first the acquaintanceship of all who have written of
him, from a Thiers to a Madame de Rémusat. Each will
have a man of his own, made up of Bonaparte and *ego*.
Bonaparte *and* Thiers make Thiers'; Bonaparte *and* de
Rémusat make de Rémusat's. I must make mine of Bonaparte—*i.e.*, all their Bonapartes—and myself. It will take
a long time; after all the ingredients are thrown into the
caldron, from "poisoned toad" to "Tartar's lip," there
must be a deal of stirring and fire-poking before the image
will emerge; but finally come it will, my Bonaparte, my
veritable little corporal, and in him I will believe, though an
archbishop in sacerdotal robes tells me there never lived a
Bonaparte.   Nowhere more than in the study of history is it
needful to "put yourself in his place"—*i.e.*, to carry to the
making of an image of the person whose form you seek to
confront, those general and common ingredients which go
to make up each man. When you have carried to him that

much of yourself which is common to you both, you will, by this, be qualified to detect that in him which is himself strictly, and not yourself ; and so to a man you will add the individuality of this man, and have what you seek.   Carlyle carried Carlyle to the making of his Cromwell, doubtless ; and in this way he got for himself a complete Cromwell—wart and all—to his mind.   Taine thinks Cromwell's Cromwell is Carlyle's Cromwell, and largely because they are, in his view, interchangeable words.   Nowhere more than in history does it " take a thief to catch a thief."

III.

Why shall we study history ?   For so laborious and perilous a process as that I have depicted, there must be much motive and imperative motive.

I would have the study of history not an end, but a means to an end.   I would study history, first, in order to know myself.

" The proper study of mankind is man."   Know thyself is the first mandate of a sound and comprehensive philosophy.   Yet true self-knowledge is never to be come at by burrowing in the narrow limit of our own individual thoughts, feelings, and experience.   We must, in order to truly see ourselves, stand before the great mirror humanity, and in its all-reflecting focus behold our own proper individuality.   Taine says " all history is but the history of the heart."   We find ourselves surrounded by humanity, we find ourselves humanity, and of humanity we know less than of anything else. We have studied history wrongly, and it has yielded us only date and event, deed and career. Let us study it rightly, and it will yield us true self-knowledge, true sympathy with others. Here, as elsewhere, it is "the spirit that quickeneth." Goethe said, "It is the spirit in which we act which is the great thing." It is the spirit in which we study which is the great thing. Does history hold a hero for us? Let us love him boundlessly but wisely; if we praise him, let our praise be abundant but understanding, as was Heine's, when he says, in explanation of seeming to praise Bonaparte in praising his deeds, "I never praise the dead, but the human soul whose garment the deed is, and history is nothing but the soul's old wardrobe." I would study history that I may be wise—wise with a sympathetic wisdom born of much and reverent contact with my brother and sister humanity.

"Knowledge comes, but wisdom lingers, and we linger on the shore ;
    And the individual withers, and the world is more and more."

I would study history rightly that my knowledge may be fused with wisdom. I would stand among the men and women of the past in order that I may stand among the men and women of the present—an individual ; not caught, and absorbed, and lost in the great world-current, for "wisdom lingers !"

And, in the second place, I would study history in order to make my standing firmer in religious faith. In these days of ebb and quicksand, when agnosticism rears its stone-wall in front of faith, and writes upon it in black letters the end-all and the be-all of all knowing, the unknowable, we have need to go where God is to confirm our faith in Him.

And God is in history ; He is there because the human soul is there. "Take thy shoes from off thy feet, for this is holy ground." Turn the pages reverently, for, as Carlyle says, "all history is the Bible."

These two reasons why I would study history come first in rank. After these come all other benefits which the intellect gets to itself in any exercise of its faculties ; in no other pursuit can these be greater. The exploration of no science can be, in all ways, so profitable as must be the science of humanity.

The science of matter is a very noble pursuit. To wrench from the ores of the earth, the treasures of the sea, the elements of the air, the secret of their functions and their affinities, the laws of their being, the springs of their action —this is very noble and very good. But it ends where it begins—in matter ; and matter is matter and not man, despite the Darwins, and Tyndalls, and Huxleys ; and one may know all that is to be known about matter and nothing that need be known about man.

The science of astronomy is very grand. To make acquaintance with the steadfast stars, to know their times and seasons, their comings and their goings—to learn their hidden looks by distance-killing telescopes, so that each feature is familiar, must make one feel a sense of more than mundane importance, and a sense of fellowship more than mortal. Yet, after all, if an astronomer do nothing but gaze at the stars, he is only a star-gazer. But the science of humanity—what limit is there here? Here is a labyrinth for learning, an ocean for genius, a cathedral for worship !

The most transcendent genius should occupy itself with history. It does indeed, in a sense, for the loftiest reaches

of the loftiest minds have always been in the study of man ;
but I would have the abstract psychology of these great
ones made concrete.   I would that Goethe's Faust had been
a more solid figure in history—*i.e.*, I would that all the
genius, and soul exploration, and experience, with all the
transcendent learning that went to its making, might have
turned into some historic evolution—that of Charlemagne,
for instance.   What a history would that have been !

Is there not a yearning in these dumb, eloquent faces
which confront us from the pages of history to give us the
lesson they learned here, which shall move us to accept their
teaching ?   Teaching concerning our relations with each
other in this present, where we must briefly play our part,
nobly or ignobly ; teaching that shall train us for that long
hereafter, within whose dim recesses even now is set a waiting messenger, biding his time to beckon, and whose beckoning we must one day surely follow into those same silent
corridors of the past.   Do not these, the departed great
ones, speaking all the more eloquently because the clogging
web of irrelevant detail has dropped away and left bare and
prominent to our vision only the vital and important—do
not these teach us something that we need to learn ?

There is a science which, whether in little or in much,
pursued by patient industry, by educated imagination, by
rigorous conscience, shall teach us, of all things that it concerns us to know—history—the true and proper study of
humanity !

OLD ROME AND NEW FRANCE

OLD ROME AND NEW FRANCE.

I.

THERE is a notion of the Middle Ages which is common and which is false—a notion which looks upon them as ten centuries of starless midnight, wherein the world lay asleep —as good as dead.   A tunnel of time, one thousand years long, through which humanity rumbled blindly in an emigrant train, the last sky-rockets of the Roman Empire flaring up at one end, the first sunbeams of the Renaissance shining in at the other—and no light between—the no-account period of history.

We are all liable to have notions until we get knowledge ; but if any of us hold this one, it should be corrected before we enter upon mediæval studies.   It seems to me that this period is not suggestively named when called the Middle Ages, nor accurately named when called the Dark Ages, but that both suggestion and accuracy combine in that view which denominates it as a Twilight Age.   That period which elapses before sunrise, that period which elapses after sunset, and all that interval between when moon and star ray forth their multitudinous lances of silver light, waging successful warfare with the cannonade of serried cloud—these periods we find indeed dim, but not wholly unlit ; obscure, but not impenetrable.   Such a night as this is that of the Middle Ages.

The importance of acquaintance with this period is, by the ordinary student, greatly underestimated. Yet it is emphatically the seed-time of all that succeeds. The skilful florist, if he wishes to insure the germination of precious seed, casts it into pots of prepared earth, then sets these pots away in the brooding darkness of his hothouse, and there keeps them until the delicate sprout above the earth assures him that germination is well under way. Growth takes place in the night. He who would approach history in the true attitude of a scientist, a psychologist, a student of Providence, must concern himself with its seed-time, its time of sprouting and of early growth. As much as is the importance of study of this period underestimated, so greatly is its interest unappreciated. He who, with some true conception of what the mediæval period is to after-times, shall but cross the threshold of its study, will, once within, proceed along those dim-lit aisles with an interest as much exceeding that of more brilliant subsequent ages as does the fascination of the mysterious, pregnant, prodigy-filled night exceed that of the glaring day! Let us, then, cross this threshold.

By one bold exercise of your imagination place yourself with me within the vestibule of mediæval time. Above the lintel of the door we enter is written in blood-red letters the date—476. This vestibule is long—three centuries lie between its doorway and the massive portal of the temple proper yonder, on which flames forth, in letters of gilt, the date 800.

Here in this antechamber the twilight deepens; a side light radiates fitfully here and there, but our way is mainly featured to us by the rays that issue, the one from a red sunset behind, the other from a rising moon in front—the ensanguined light that lingers in the wake of Rome that was, the ruddy gold that parts the clouds where France shall be. In the fifth century of modern time the Roman Empire had grown cancerous upon the world. The iron of its blood—its Julius, its Trajan, its Aurelius—had run out. The virus of a Nero, a Domitian, a Caligula had mingled with the watery serum of a Heliogabalus and an Augustulus, and had brought mortal sickness. There was need of surgery. Then nature, that great nature which, in history as elsewhere, is Providence, arose, and with the sword of Hun and Goth cut out this cancer which was poisoning the race. With the contented retirement to his Lucullan villa of the little, bribed Augustus—Romulus Augustulus, too small to fight and not too big to buy—the last effigy of Cæsar flitted from the stage of history, and Rome, the monopolist, the tyrant, the disease, vanished from the body politic.

[Surely, I need not interject a word of tribute to that glorious Rome which still lives with transmigrated life, that other Rome, that unparalleled product into which all the ages of the world had entered as contributors, in that fashion which the ages have. For human history is nothing but one ceaseless flow of cause into effect, and of effect into cause. There is nothing but which is consequent. You and I are but the consequents of a vast tangle of antecedents in all time before. And but for Rome, that stupendous concrete of wealth and culture and intellect of eighteen centuries ago, it had not been the same with you and me to-day. This Rome, vastly differing from that othe Rome that was extinguished, died only with such death as good

things have—a death which is transition—and in dying
bequeathed her rich arterial blood to all the ages.]

One glance, then, at this flickering sunset sky of Rome
(its embers will light many a watch-fire of the future),
and we must face about and thread our way as best we can
along this dim vestibule of the Twilight Age, by such
radiance as glimmers from a moon struggling through
cumulous clouds before us.

In its focus stands a figure, the figure in political history
of the next three centuries, upon which we must fasten our
attention—the figure of Clovis, initial name of French
Empire.   Ten years after the so-called extinction of the
Western Empire of the Romans in the deliverance up of
his little, brief authority by the puny Augustulus to
Odoacer, there ruled over the Roman territory of Gaul,
with the title, some say, of the King of the Romans, a
Roman patrician, Syagrius.   This fact alone discovers to us
how life lingered in the moribund members of the ruined
empire.   With less start than, it would seem, Syagrius
had, many a man had beforetime usurped the empire and
ruled the world.   We may say that the time for all such
usurpations of Roman Empire was now gone by.   But we
can maintain this position only after the event.   It took
but the returning figure of Napoleon upon the shore of
France, after his banishment, to rally round him his army
and restore to him his empire, dislodging from the throne
of France that ancient dynasty which, in the emperor's brief
absence, had been reseated there.   Some one has said that
such was the magic of Napoleon's name, that it needed but
the sight of his cocked hat, erected on the soil of France,
to strike terror to the heart of Europe.   In this closing fifth

century the Roman eagles had not wholly lost their power
to stir up Roman souls ; witness the Senator Boethius, his
father-in-law, Symmachus, and their colleagues, found
guilty, after that date, of loyalty to that ancient standard.
Nor was the subjugation and unity of the barbarian
Odoacer's kingdom so assured as to leave no room for a
reasonable hope in one who should aspire to restore the
Roman Empire to the Romans, of allies from barbarian
tribes. Syagrius, the son of a Roman hero, would seem to
have been such an one. He was exceedingly popular among
his countrymen in the Gallic territory over which he ruled ;
nor was he less so among barbarian allies, whom, by his
superiority, he both awed and attracted. He represented
to the rude nations about him what was awful, and admirable, and wholly beyond their reach in the traditions and
manners of that Rome which, by numbers only, they had
conquered. Here, we might say, was opportunity for a
most successful *coup d'état* by this illustrious, powerful,
and accomplished Roman. We can give no conclusive
reason why it could not have happened except that it did
not. We can only be wise after the event. The panorama
of history unrolls itself always to surprised spectators.
Always " it is the unexpected that happens." Not Syagrius,
in this fifth century of time, but a roving, barbarian chieftain, is the coming man.

Clovis—our modern for Chodowig, mighty warrior—was
the son of Childeric, king of that branch of the Frankish
barbarians whose settlements lay along the river Sala, or
Yssel, hence their distinctive appellation, Salian Franks.
The Franks had figured in history for several centuries.
They were no strangers to the Roman world. From the

beginning, when the hero-god of Germany, Arminius, beat back the Roman legions under Varus, this valorous race had, by one or another of its tribes, won the respect and sometimes fear of the Romans, in the varying character of enemies, allies, or subjects. The eminent qualities of this race were courage and independence. It was from their inconquerable passion for freedom that they won their name —Franks, freemen. Even in their relation to their chief they were rather allies than subjects.*

Childeric, the father of Clovis, was a wild and wilful man, whose youthful madnesses out-Franked the Franks, and provoked them, with characteristic democracy, to ignore his kingship and banish him to the court of a neighboring king, where, in good care, he might find space for repentance. It does not appear that he occupied himself exclusively with this wholesome but bitter spiritual exercise. Childeric seems to have anticipated the later French character, whose law of life lay in the phrase of the Bourbon courtiers, "*Je m'amuse!*" He had the national instinct, "*pour passer le temps,*" and in this experience passed the time principally in making love to Bosnia, the wife of the open-hearted King of Thuringia. She, for her part, found no difficulty in falling duly "in love" with this fascinating French exile, and when the Franks recalled

---

* The famous story of the vase of Soissons illustrates the independent attitude they maintained as soldiers to their general and as subjects to their king. After the first victory of Clovis, a rare and exquisite vase was among the spoils. This Clovis set aside for himself. But a soldier seeing him do this stepped forth from the ranks, and, exclaiming, "You shall have nothing but what comes to you by lot," struck the vase and shivered it to atoms.

their monarch to his place, Bosnia incontinently left Thu-
ringian bed and board, declaring, with an emancipation of
soul which it takes the nineteenth century to equal, that
" had she found a man more beautiful than Childeric, he
should have been her choice !"

The saying that " the mother makes the man" seems to
find illustration in the character of Clovis. Bosnia was the
regulation mother for a conqueror, and she bequeathed him
the quality which he needed as equipment for his bloody and
unscrupulous career—unswerving selfishness, which allows
no foolish conscience to impede the course of its passion, be
that passion for a kingdom or—a king. So fine an irony
has history, that that which makes the shame of its wives
makes the glory of its kings !

Clovis succeeded to the kingdom of his father at the age
of fifteen, if, indeed, a strip of Rhineland and a band of
followers can be called a kingdom. Clovis was poor, but
he was young ; his resources were small, but his valor
boundless ; his followers few, but congenial.

Six years elapse, after the accession of Clovis to his
throne, before the first great event of his career writes itself
indelibly upon the page of history. At this moment of
world-history the situation in Gaul—modern France—was
as follows : Its north-eastern portion was the territory of
Syagrius. Its central and south-western lands were included in the great barbarian kingdom of the Visigoths,
which extended also across the Pyrenees and took in part of
Spain. The small sea-coast strip remaining in the north-
west was called Armorica, and was virtually independent.
The more considerable south-eastern lands, which bordered
Italy, were possessed by the Burgundians, who also ruled

themselves. To the east of Burgundy, along that region
of the Rhine, an indeterminate host—that barbarian con-
glomerate called suggestively the Allemanni (All-men)—lay
crouching with gleaming eyes, biding their time for a
spring across the river barrier. And above them, farther
along the beach, Clovis, the young Frank chieftain, roamed
restlessly up and down, with his congenial followers, and
cast glances full of speculation across to Gallic lands. We
may well pause here to take in this situation, in this
momentous decade, between the years of our Lord 476 and
486. All eyes that glance on mediæval history must turn
thither and fix an affrighted gaze upon these ten years, in
which the future of the world is pending. Visigoth and, behind him, Vandal on the west ; Ostrogoth on the south ; Allemanni on the east, each stretching neck and straining eye
—all turning a fascinated gaze upon the basilisk Syagrius.
He is the cocked hat of Napoleon to them. And all this
time Clovis whistles softly up and down the hither Rhine,
planning, in the waiting for performance ; dreaming, in
delay of deed, "dreams no mortal ever dared to dream
before." But finally the spell is broken. The contest
begins, and Clovis strides forth to throw down before
Syagrius the gauntlet of battle.

II.

"In the manner and almost in the language of chivalry,"
says Gibbon, "Clovis defied Syagrius and called him to
combat. Syagrius haughtily accepted the challenge, and
met him in the vicinity of the ancient city Soissons."

Tragic ground, this, for France ! For if the Soissons of the fifth be not identical with the Sedan of the nineteenth century, the two are sufficiently related to suggest a striking reflection. For it was here, in the year 486, that Clovis swung his battle-axe victorious over Roman heads, and wrote in Roman blood the birthday of French Empire ! And it was here, in 1870, that the last French emperor delivered up his sword, and William of Prussia wrote in Frenchmen's blood the death-day of French Empire !

The victory of Clovis at Soissons put an end to Roman rule in Gaul. Syagrius fled to the Visigothic court and disappeared from view. Clovis filled his place in Gaul, and came to view for all time.

We of the nineteenth know now that at this moment, in the fifth century, Clovis, by his victory over Syagrius, had laid the corner-stone of French Empire. To us he already appears a hero, having taken that first step which costs, and after which all the others come as a matter of course. But nothing was farther from the fact. This first step of Clovis led the way to others more costly. What he had gained he must hold, and that was not a matter of a day's fight. A difficulty more subtle than the barbarian mind had been accustomed to grapple with now arose to threaten Clovis.

The Roman world had long since been nominally Christian. Roman Gaul was extremely Christian, as we shall see, and Roman Gaul, however it may perforce submit to a political master not Roman, had serious scruples in submitting to a pagan master not Christian. Thus the situation became very difficult for Clovis. Not being one which the battle-axe could adjust, he was hardly equal to it. These Romish priests, with their wonderful learning, and

language, and polished dignity, were more than a match for
our lusty Frank.   Yet Clovis was not without diplomacy ;
and two circumstances assisted him to meet the emergency.

The first of these circumstances was the circumstance of
sectarianism.   A split in the opposing party, as we of
to-day know, is often the determining factor in the fight.
Such a split had occurred long before the time of Clovis,
and now had yawned into irreconcilable divergence.   Thus
early in the history of the Christian era are we called upon
to witness the tremendous power of sect, as a force in the
causation of events.   Already in the fifth century was the
half-admiring pagan world invited to "see how these
Christians hate each other !"

The great sect of those days, and that with which alone
we have to do, was that of the Arian heresy.   All who
indorsed the doctrine of Arius were considered heterodox,
and were known as Arians, while those untainted with this
heresy were deemed the orthodox, and were called by that
glorious but so often misapplied name of Catholics.   A good
follower of Augustine in the fifth century could no more
fellowship a good follower of Arius than could a rigid disciple of Calvin in our century fellowship one of Chunder Sen.

Now, the Roman Gauls were fiercely orthodox, while all
around them, the Visigothic, Ostrogothic, and Burgundian
converts to Christianity, were fiercely Arian ; and these
two divisions of the early Church hated each other most
cordially.   In this way was Clovis helped out of his
dilemma, for the hatred of his orthodox Roman subjects of
their Christian but Arian neighbors was quite as great as
was their repugnance to a pagan ruler.   They may even
have thought the latter the least of two evils.   Thus

was prevented alliance with those neighbors against the
conquering Clovis, who threatened the barbarian nations in
Gaul with the same political ruin he had brought to the
Romans. How lasting would have been this prevention of
such allied resistance to him, or what might have come
about from this complication, it were profitless to conjecture.
We can only follow the course of events, and see how the
matter took care of itself.

The course of events is just now the course of Clovis, and
the next thing we have to chronicle in his career is also the
second which served to assist him in meeting the situation
in which we find him after his conquest of Roman Gaul,
the circumstance of his marriage.

More than one woman goes to the making of one man,
or, if not, the man lacks something of being finished.
The mother makes the man, perhaps, but the wife manufact-
ures him. Sometimes the wife, in her manufacture, con-
firms the making of the mother, sometimes counteracts it.
The case of Clovis was that of counteraction, for it appears
certain that the influence of Clotilda, the wife, went far
toward nullifying the influence of her mother-in-law. She
seems, as much as possible, to have been the opposite in
character of her husband's mother.

In the first place, Clotilda was a Christian and orthodox,
and she set herself to the task of her husband's conversion
with Catholic zeal.

I am not informed of the circumstances of the courtship
of Clovis. It occurs to me with force, however, that these
recently-acquired, troublesome Catholic subjects of his may
have acted the part of match-makers to a very great extent.
At any rate, we can all perceive the significance to them of

the marriage of their pagan monarch with this Catholic princess, and how far it would go toward reconciling him to them, as being now in a hopeful way for conversion to their faith.

A painful suspicion also whispers itself in my ear, suggesting that in Clovis the passion of the lover may have conspired with the policy of the ruler in the wooing of his bride. Be that as it may, the Roman Catholic clergy now adhered to Clovis with hopeful loyalty. The pious hope of priest and wife was not rewarded earlier than the date of the next great battle of Clovis, in the year 496, ten years after the battle of Soissons. This encounter was with a foe vastly different from that of ten years before, but its result hardly second in importance.

III.

We have already spoken of the Allemannic tribes as menacing the eastern frontier of Gaul. They were but the advance guard of untold, almost unimaginable savage hordes that swarmed within those northern wilds of Germany which Rome had disdained to penetrate. It was this force which Clovis had now to confront. Had they succeeded in the contest and pushed their way over the dead bodies of these Franks, to fill again the place of Syagrius which Clovis had won, unnumbered myriads must have rushed down from those dark forests of the north to fill, in turn, the places thus left vacant, and the establishment of the new empire must have been indefinitely retarded or disastrously changed.

Near the present site of Cologne these two barbarian tribes, whom Gibbon calls the fiercest of the many then in view, confronted each other, to settle between them this momentous question. The battle raged furiously and variously, but at last fortune seemed to perch upon the Allemannic banner. The gods of the Franks were invoked to aid, but appeared to be otherwise engaged. Then, when defeat seemed certain, in that extremity which brings each man begging to the Almighty One, Clovis, the long-resisting, in true barbaric heartiness spoke out to Clotilda's God, praying for victory and vowing Him the service of a Christian ever after might he but win this fight. From this instant the tide of battle turned. Fresh vigor flew into the arms of the retreating Franks. They turned upon their pursuers, and fought, with fanatic frenzy, the battle over again. The Allemanni were slaughtered in vast numbers, and their nation completely subdued. The dead bodies of their slain formed an effectual barrier against invasion of remoter savage hordes. The eastern frontier of Gaul was temporarily assured.

A second consequence of this battle, greater even than the settlement of an eastern frontier, was the conversion of Clovis.*

* It were a profitless, perhaps painful, inquiry to seek to ascertain the true nature of this so-called conversion. We may well suspend our criticism, and temper skepticism with faith—we who have said that we

> ". . . believe that in all ages
> Every human heart is human,
> That in even savage bosoms
> There are longings, yearnings, strivings,
> For the good they comprehend not."

The barbarian chieftain is told the story of the death and sufferings of

So Clovis keeps his vow and changes masters. He is received into the Holy Catholic Church and—because he is a Catholic, not an Arian—is hailed by the Pope with the title of "Most Christian!" With three thousand of his Franks following he goes behind Remigius to the baptismal font. Here is exercise for imagination. What a picture does it hang before us! Clovis, fresh from the field of battle, with his elated soldiers, bending massive forms before the mitred bishop in the grand Cathedral of Rheims. That long-haired monarch—for long hair was the distinction of the German kings—those fair-skinned, fair-haired warriors, suppliant, while Remigius uplifts the cross before them, and, in sonorous Latin, commands for it their homage—"*Mitis depone colla, Sicamber! Adora quod incendisti, incende quod adorâsti!*" Truly new times this for Clovis, to bow meekly anywhere, to anything!

Christ. Missing the meaning of that matchless tale, his impulsive heart swells with indignation, and, clasping his battle-axe, he cries out, "Would I had been there at the head of my valiant Franks! I would have avenged His injuries." Yet, I think, it is only we who smile at this barbaric fervor. I think the patient Christ, who wept but never laughed over the creature He died to save, would likelier lay a gentle hand upon that outstretched arm of Clovis, discerning, as He alone can do, the unconscious worship in that generous heart!

Led, as a child, by the bishop to the Cathedral of Rheims, Clovis, his savage nature impressed and elated by the splendor of its adornments, asks, "Is this the kingdom of God, of which I am become an heir?"

> Then spake the gray barbarian,
> Lower than a Christian child!

And Remigius answers, "No; but it is the road thither!" And there the shadow of Hildebrand was cast before!

But the cross is adored—at least in form—the pagan idols
which have been worshipped are burned, and the end for
which wife and priest have long been waiting is attained.
Clovis is a Christian, and his victorious career is fairly
under way. The sword in one hand, the cross in the other,
he is prepared for any emergency of conquest. He is now
at length ready for his third and final move in the game
which wins the new empire. This is his victory at Poitiers
over the Visigoths in Gaul.

IV.

The Visigoths are intensely Arian ; Clovis is intensely
Catholic. Arianism is a heresy—a shocking heresy, and
Clovis feels now that it is his duty to rebuke this scandalous
schism in the Church. He will fight the Visigoths and
expel them from Gaul. Thus does his piety supply him
pretext for a conquest " in fresh fields and pastures new !"
The preparations of Clovis for this last great campaign
have all the character of a crusade. He summons his
prelates and princes to a council at Paris, whither he
has removed the seat of government from Soissons. Here
he advises with them on the best means of extirpation
of this lamentable heresy from the territory of Gaul. He
has a word for both. He says : " It grieves me that
the Arians possess as yet the fairest lands of Gaul. Let
us march against them with the aid of God, and, having
punished the heretics, we will possess and divide their
lands !"
His warriors all fall in with this disinterested plan, and

swear that until the Arians are punished their beards shall remain uncut ! *

When the fires of fanaticism are once kindled every circumstance adds fuel to the flames. The Crusaders set forth amid a shower of auspicious portents ; their journey to the battle-field is one series of miraculous omens. Their route is indicated by a meteor ; the unknown fording-place of a river by the passage through before them of a white hart of supernatural beauty. Alaric II. and his Visigothic hosts are paralyzed with the rumors which precede the advent of the enemy. Under these circumstances the army of Clovis closes in around them and reduces them to speedy submission. They fly, and Clovis pursues them ; until they disappear behind the Pyrenees, he gives no quarter. Thus ends the Visigothic supremacy in Gaul. Thus are the hated heretics punished and their fair lands possessed.

This third great battle on the field of Poitiers, in the year 507, consummated substantially the Frankish conquest of Gaul. And with this ends our concern in the career of Clovis. Of his treaty with the little free Armorica ; of his contests, finally ending in victory, with the more obstinate and troublesome Burgundy ; of his indiscriminate flinging hither and yon among his too presuming kindred and dukes of the formidable *Francesca*, by way of filling up his time, we have naught to say. All these things hap-

---

* Clotilda, the Christian wife, stands by and counsels her lord to promise God a monastery after the accomplishment of this pious purpose, and Clovis, filled with devotion, seizes his favorite battle-axe (which, after the manner of the swords of heroes, has a name as individual as its owner), and hurling it from him, exclaims, " There, where my Francisca shall stick, will I build a house to God !"

pened, as he who runs may read. Just one hundred years
after the sack of Rome by Alaric the Goth, in the year
510, Clovis received from the eastern empire the title—
the ultimatum, it seems, of his ambition—of Consul.
Gibbon says`: " On the solemn day (of coronation) the
monarch of Gaul, placing a diadem upon his own head,
was invested, in the Church of St. Martin, with the purple tunic and mantle. From thence he proceeded on
horseback to the Cathedral of Tours, and as he passed
through the streets scattered with his own hand a donation
of gold and silver to the joyful multitude, who incessantly
repeated their acclamations of *Consul !* and *Augustus !*"

Strange thing, this human nature, with its misapplied
magnanimity and irrelevant vanity ! Clovis, a year before
his death, with the territory of the Visigoths, the Burgundians, the Romans in Gaul, and diverse barbarian tribes
beneath his feet, the crown of a new empire on his head,
looks not forward to the future of his kindred Franks, but
backward to the past of his alien Romans. The name, the
fame, the future grandeur of the nebulous new empire does
not compare with the faded grandeur of the starry old.
He would rather stand, dressed in a little brief authority—
ghostly and fictitious though it be—among the buried
Cæsars, than build for himself the solid fame of founder of
that empire which subdued the empire of the Cæsars.
Sweeter to him the cry from pusillanimous Roman throats
of Consul ! Consul ! and Augustus ! though he knew it but
the forced utterance of cunning policy, than all the thun-
derous vociferations of his lusty Franks of Clovis ! Clovis !
Emperor of France ! Truly, a lame and impotent conclusion.

The next year after his coronation as Consul, in the year
511 of the Christian era, having attained the age of only
forty-five years, after a reign of thirty years, Clovis died.

And here we part company with the founder of the French
Empire. Our knowledge of him as an individual is too
limited to justify a discussion of his character. We leave him
as we find him, unequivocally a conqueror, " cast," as Hallam says, " in the true mould of conquerors, and may justly
be counted among the first of his class both for the splendor and the guiltiness of his ambition." He is conspicuous
only as the figure which emerges from the chaotic politics
of that ruinous epoch, assuming the *rôle* of Founder of the
New State. In this character his main equipment is that
of his battle-axe. We discern in him little of constructive
genius to mould the state after he has founded it.

We cannot depart from this vestibule of mediæval time
without a glance at another figure, whose name we have
already mentioned—a figure most independent and conspicuous, and at this moment of world-history most significant of
the old, as is that of Clovis of the new. We must turn to
that red sky of Rome, if we would look on him, for he
stands bathed in its last glow—Boethius! last Roman worthy
to hold rank with Cato and with Cicero. Yet not only
by that departing ray of Rome is he conspicuous to our
eyes. He shines with light self-centred—that diamond-
shine which issues from the fiery particle within,

> " The light that never was on land or sea,
> The consecration and the poet's dream,"

that ray which makes him common to all climes and times,
an immortal citizen in the commonwealth of genius and of

faith. There is little in the personality of Clovis to interest us. He has no magnetism save that which the iron of his battle-axe may lend. But the tender gaze of all generations is fixed with loyal love on the figure of Boethius. We can never learn enough about him. No other could be contrived to oppose to the figure of Clovis which should more vividly discover the contrast of forces which contend for mastery in the conflict of the ages, and none more nakedly representative of the forces at work in this mingling of the old with the new at this chaotic period.

Clovis stands to us as representative of the red young blood, the cordy young muscle that must vitalize the shrunken veins of time and nerve the arm of humanity for the work of construction of new political empire in the state that is to be. The lusty young Frank has little of equipment—nor needs he more—for the task that is set him, than that same bright battle-axe along whose whetted edge we see red blood-drops globing. He stands all unconscious that in the mirror of one face are seen the shades of all Rome's Cæsars in their purple, and in the mirror of its opposite face are seen the forecast images of the Louis and the Napoleons, the Richeliens and the Bismarcks—the shadows cast before of coming events and coming men ! Boethius stands to us as a parting summary of all that was best of Rome—as senator, as patrician, as poet, as philosopher. When Clovis was crowned Consul at Tours, Boethius was already Consul in the court of Theodoric at Rome, and *princeps senatus.* But too true a Roman to wear Roman honors in a Gothic court, he was soon found guilty of Roman patriotism—*i.e.*, of Gothic treason—and the court was exchanged for a dungeon. But we bless the dungeon of Boe-

thius as we bless the cell of Bunyan. For from it came
that golden volume which poured enduring consolation into
all those ages. Beloved of Alfred, beloved of Charlemagne,
beloved of Dante, called, during those dark, laboring ages
the Augustine of philosophy, Boethius comes down to us the
noblest Roman of them all, since from those prison walls
could issue strains like this : "Nobility is in no other
respect good than as it imposes an obligation upon its pos-
sessors not to degenerate from the merit of their ancestors !
If you are not therefore esteemed illustrious from your
own worth, you can derive no real splendor from the merits
of others." There speaks the nobleman, whether sixth
century patrician, in whose veins coursed the purplest blood
of Rome's most noble families, or nineteenth century Dem-
ocrat—a grand old gardener at the gate,

>   ". . . too proud to care from whence he came !"

Unconsciously this great soul sounds the trumpet notes
of the truth which in all those slow, sad ages struggled to
be heard above the clash and discord, and which now rings
joy-bells in our glorious nineteenth century ; but he, its
noble voicer, in that darkest time heard but the tolling of
death-knells, and looked sadly backward to Rome's freedom, and counted

>   " Sorrow's crown of sorrow
>   In remembering happier things."

We may fancy the stern face of the passionless Genius of
History, as she stands upon some Alpine summit between
France and Italy, at the close of this fifth century, to relax
a little, half in pity, half in mirth, at the parody of great-

ness which her puppets play. Yet, as she gazes on the perfect plan which through all these puppet-plays goes on to its supreme fulfilment, we may behold a gleam of fathomless content, restored to her countenance, and may perhaps catch the words of that epilogue which, after the play is over, she lingers to say.

With one hand to the south, she exclaims : " Go ! thou imperial Rome ; take thou henceforth thy place among the deeds which have been *done*. Die, as such deeds must die. Imperishable fact among the facts of history, recede now into the past, thy future dwelling-place ! I would thou could'st go queenly, as thou cam'st and long hast stood, the purple trailing royally and sweeping past with tragic funereal mien. But since the comedy must come, and then the farce, make now an end ! Thy errand with the world is done. The time was set, and now the hour strikes. Farewell, thou glorious Rome ! Thy glories cover well thy guilt ; thy graces cover well thy shame. The world has gained from thee its priceless gains, its luminous examples, its enduring warnings. Fare thee well !"

And with a right hand to the north, she says : " Welcome, thou infant France, born from the death of Rome ! Two hours are set for thee, as for all things human ; the first strikes now. That other hour is set, and it will come. 'Twixt that and this lies all thy errand with the waiting world. For those that pass away I have a smile ; for those that come, a tear. And over thee, yet in thy swaddling-clothes, while I discern the life that is to be, I bend, and with a solitary tear baptize thee—*France !*"

CHARLEMAGNE

CHARLEMAGNE.

AT the conclusion of the eighth century we find upon
the throne of Clovis a man, son of an usurper, called by his
kindred subjects Karl, by his alien subjects Carolus ;
endowed by nature with superb physical gifts, with a clear
and curious intellect, a swift, inexorable will, a fervent
heart, and a religious spirit ; further furnished by inheritance with the dominant empire of the world, and with
the following of his father's veteran armies, while the
Genius of Conquest beckons on this side and on that. Thus
the facts of history set forth, in the eighth century,
this monarch Charlemagne. At the conclusion of the
Middle Ages we behold this same Karl standing in a radiant
flood of fiction, with the aspect of a demi-god !

Poetry has been defined as the highest truth, but the
poets have done little for history. If the singers had been
content to let Arthur alone, we might now have had a history of him. Poets rush in where historians fear to tread ;
after idyls, no history !

In the latter half of the Middle Ages the poets, in the
dearth of heroes, got hold of Charlemagne, and made him
realize to them their ideal man. The monks got hold of
Charlemagne, and made him realize to them their ideal
saint. The knights got hold of Charlemagne, and made
him realize to them their ideal chevalier : and so it came

about that Charlemagne stood as a name for everything which in those ages could be conceived the best in humanity—summing up in one every possible grace and gift of monarch and man, hero and saint—realizing to each ideal perfection ! But the idealized, of nations as of individuals, are subject to the same law which governs the idealizer, the law of reaction ; and to this rule, we fear, there are no exceptions. With the early sunbeams of the Renaissance the lovely legend-mists which had hung around the form of Charlemagne were, not indeed dispelled, but cut, and when the fresh breeze of advancing day set in were lifted for the image. And now, in the high noon of our scientific century, but little enchantment remains to the picture, save that which distance always lends. The kaiser of the eighth century unconsciously set the fashion for his own treatment in the nineteenth, when he fell upon the Irmensul of the Saxons, and, razing the temple, stripped the idol of its gold and gems, and bore it, naked and unadorned, to the monastery which was at once the treasury and the library of the Middle Ages. Disillusioned is this man to us, but not yet destroyed. There are verities in this mass of fiction which may be eliminated.

There was a man named Eginhardus, and he was secretary to the Kaiser Karl. The secretary wrote the memoirs of his monarch, and, making due allowance for the partiality of friend, or devotion of subject, or vanity of biographer, we have left a personal history so simple and direct that it commands our credence. From this mainly, with a few other ancient chronicles and comments, rather than from any modern researches, do we make some brief sketch of this luminous figure in mediæval history.

I.

First let us look at this man of whom we propose to speak. And here we will let Eginhardus speak for us. Behold, first, his frontispiece photograph. A figure whose height was seven times the length of his foot; whose heavy body was well supported by massive limbs ; a round head, hair beautiful to look upon, a nose of more than middle size, enormous eyes, large and lively, writes the secretary (" with the seeming of a lion's, and shining like carbuncles," adds a curt old chronicle), a countenance joyful and vivacious, sitting and standing like a king, walking with a firm, quick step ; a man of splendid presence, according to all accounts. An old song thus puts it, in obsolete German :

> " Karl war den Rosenglich !"
> 　　*　　　　*　　　　*　　　　*

And sums up as follows :

> " Ich waiz wol das von wibe
> 　Nie wart, noch nimmer werden sol
> 　Ein man so mannig tugend vol."

> (" Karl was like a rose !"
> 　*　　*　　*　　*　　*　　*
> " I well know that to women
> 　So sweet a hero-man
> 　Ne'er lived, nor ever can !")

Let now this figure stand before you clad, as Eginhardus dresses him, in his short linen drawers and his long linen drawers : in his linen waistcoat, over which is drawn

a coat trimmed with fur ; throw upon his herculean shoulders a Venetian mantle ; hang at his side his good and well-
beloved sword Joyeuse ; place his right hand upon its golden
hilt—*et voila !* the Kaiser Karl in his every-day clothes.
For the secretary gives us to understand he is not in
the least " dressed up. " He has fine clothes, however ; but
he keeps them like the careful man he is, bringing them
forth when he goes visiting to Rome, or something of that
sort. Then he shines from diademed head to jewelled foot
with all the splendor heart could wish. Mostly French
splendor, too, for Karl was a clear Frenchman, despising
all alien finery, and never would he adopt a foreign fashion. A man of superb health which no bad habits under-
mined, we are assured. He despised drunkenness, though
not an abstainer (like Charles XII. of Sweden), but moder-
ate in his drinks. In eating he was not so—runs on the
secretary—often complaining that his stomach was griev-
ously empty—a vacuum which his nature abhorred, it
would seem, for the old chronicle above quoted relates that
at one meal he would eat " a goose, two fowls, a quarter of
mutton," etc., *ad lib. !*

Not much of a society man, in the modern French line,
the secretary lets us know, but very much of a family
man, with very much of a family. I count up nine
(" wives," Hallam calls them !) successive or contemporary
proprietors of the royal heart, which is three more than
divided the affections of our amorous English Harry. Indeed, Karl, no more than Henry, was a polygamist, and
always piously interred the former incumbent of the royal
affections before wedding the next, unless, indeed, she were
unreasonably contumacious about dying, in which case a

divorce could be managed, with quite the modern improve-
ments. Only one wife—as I read the secretary—was
divorced, and that his first, whom he married to please his
mother ; as a matter of course not, therefore, pleasing himself. In every succeeding case death divorced him, leaving
him not wholly to mourn as those without hope. Concerning the remarkable mortality of these eight successive
Fatimas we have no comments from the chronicler.

Karl's children were numerous and very dear to their
father. He gave them all the advantages for learning
which he himself so diligently improved, making no difference here, it would seem, between the sons and daughters.
In appointing their after occupations, however, he was
orthodox. The boys were duly put on horseback, armed
with gun and sword, and sent to battle-field and forest for
such game as either could afford. The daughters were
duly seated at the wheel, and taught to weave what they
spun, into woollen and linen cloths, "that they might not
grow up in hateful idleness." For both boys and girls, his
children, Karl had so great affection that he never sat at
table without them, when at home, and when he took a
journey they accompanied him.

A unique procession that ! Karl, the kaiser, in his
knickerbockers and Venetian mantle, his trusty Joyeuse by
his side, upon his head his kingly helmet, seated high up
in his cumbrous chariot. His numerous sons, an ample
body-guard, cantering on either side ; the present kaiserin
and the daughters, up to date, following hard after on their
ambling pads. Quite a mediæval Vicar of Wakefield and
his family !

Eginhardus lived evidently before the times when no

man is a hero to his valet. Napoleon would have turned in his sarcophagus, if not broken sheer through and stood up, cocked hat and all, at being portrayed, as is Charlemagne, to posterity—the comfortable old gentleman, " eating a little fruit after dinner when the days were warm, drinking once, and then laying off his clothes and reposing himself for two or three hours," of a summer afternoon ! The *grand monarque* submitted to the toilette before a crowd of courtiers who came to " assist" at the ceremony of encasing the languid limbs of his most Christian majesty in silks and laces. Imagine Louis XIV. calmly pulling on his own stout shoes and stockings, and donning linen drawers and waistcoat ! Yet this was the habit of Karl, while listening to the grievances and complaints from crowds of lobbyists, and settling affairs with the same judicial dignity, we are assured, as if he were seated in the Hall of Justice.

A very vigilant man, this same napping old gentleman. All eyes and feet to his adversaries. The Saxon poets surnamed him *Velox*—Karl the Swift. Indeed, his velocity was almost a superstition with his foes ; before they dreamed he could be near he was confronting them, and their paralysis of astonishment made them the easier his victims.

As to brains, Karl was extremely clever, according to all accounts, learning what there was to learn with the greatest diligence and curiosity. Languages were the principal acquirement in those days, the mixed condition of society making necessary an acquisition of spoken tongues. The secretary tells us that his master was fluent in Latin as in his own tongue, proficient in Greek also. He also paid much attention to grammar and to rhetoric. As to his chirography, the scholars have quarrelled virtuously over the question—Could Charlemagne write? For in those days a man might read and converse in Latin and Greek and not be able to write his own name. As to the case of Charlemagne, we are content to take the word of the secretary for it—that Karl did practise penmanship, but began so late in life that he never arrived at much " enjoyment" in the art. At any rate, he made his mark, and that is more than most writers do. A very religious man was Karl, and a good Churchman of the battle-axe sort, with no special *ism*. A devout worshipper, and a great stickler for etiquette and propriety in church. Church music was a hobby, and it chimes well with the make-up of this joyous, hearty monarch that he should be a lusty singer, as was Luther. Truly devout indeed seems Karl, profiting by as well as profiting his church.

But we have indulged the secretary long enough in his fond personalities. We must turn now from the man to the monarch and the conqueror ; and here our pleasant and affectionate secretary's garrulous record will do us little service.

II.

Let us look, then, in our study of Charlemagne, away from the man to his career. If Karl was a man of qualities, he was also a man of deeds.

The first deed which belongs to the ages is, as a matter of course with so thorough a man, the consolidation of his own kingdom. Two things stood in Charlemagne's way at his accession to the throne, or, rather, two exist ences—his brother Carloman and the dukes of Aquitaine.

Carloman was, by inheritance, ruler over half the kingdom. Pepin followed the singular precedent of the Merovingian monarchs, and at his death divided his kingdom between his two sons. Here, then, at the start was a huge something for Karl to manage, and unless he had been joined by an invincible ally he might have found it the most serious thing in the whole long list of his managements, and, possibly, unmanageable. Carloman might have had as strong a fancy for a whole loaf as Carolus, and possibly Pepin's grit may have been as equally divided between his sons as was his kingdom. Had Carloman lived ! But he did not live ; or, at least, he disappeared. The critics peep and mutter here, and some of them—notably Voltaire, that *enfant terrible* to the heroes —find here a tidbit. In fact, one could wish the taking off of Carloman had been a matter less mysterious. But, in the absence of facts, there is room for the charity of the charitable as well as the suspicions of the suspicious, and we are not bound to stain the princely hand of Karl with the "eldest, primal curse," nor to hang over the history of infant France the cloud of fratricidal guilt, with which tradition has inextricably invested embryo Rome. The gist of it, to us, is that Carloman died, and his heirs disappeared, and that four years after his succession to half a throne Carolus was "elected" emperor of integral France. For Aquitaine proved not so delicate a difficulty. Its plotting dukes, representatives of the dethroned dynasty, were silenced summarily. An intermittent silence, it is true, for there was never lacking under the mane of this mettle-some Carlovingian charger the Merovingian gad-fly with its tormenting sting ; but if too small a matter to be cured, it could be endured, like any other irritation. So Carolus was "elected" over the whole of the kingdom. Nothing succeeds like success, and on this threshold of the Middle Ages it is no time to make much sacrifice of might to right. Voltaire says : " The fame of Charlemagne is one of the most eminent proofs of how the fortunate result of an unrighteous deed justifies and makes it honorable. His father was a rebel, himself an usurper."

The next pre-eminent deed of Karl's was his magnifi-cent work in Italy. The Lombards teased the popes and menaced Rome, and so the Vicar of Christ came begging to Karl, as before he had done to Pepin—for popes begged illustriously in those days, and had not yet waxed fat enough to kick at kings. Charlemagne reversed the prov-erb, and perceived " God's extremity to be man's oppor-tunity." He summoned his valiant Franks, leading them up the terrible Alps and down again on the other side with a rapidity which the Lombards could not credit, until sur-prised at Verona. They are beaten back to Pavia, capt-ured, and Pavia taken ; and the plunder—persons and pelf—Carolus, in magnificent wise, turns over to the Pope as a trifling token of affection. This is Pope Adrian, the Jonathan of this kingly David, and Charlemagne pays him now a visit, in state, between the battles, by way of a pleasure trip. First visit of the Kaiser Karl to Rome, but not his last.

A third notable deed is wrought in Spain, and this time it is a Moslem emir, in place of Christian pope, whose dilemma made Karl's excuse for new conquests. To avenge his wrongs, Karl must fight over the same ground his grand-sire fought. For it seems Charles Martel did not annihilate the Saracens. Mahometans do not die easy, even when very " sick," as we of to-day have found. Beaten back by Karl Martel, they still stand massed together to receive the grandson in his day.

The battle of Tours was fought one hundred years after the death of Mahomet. The Moslems who met Charle-magne and routed Roland on the field of Roncesvalles might themselves have heard from their grandsires the story of their encounter with his grandsire, and, in turn, some Moorish apostate might yet be living to tell of *his* grand-sire's contact with contemporaries of the great Prophet himself. The Mahometan faith was yet young and lusty, and its adherents no mean antagonists.

With his back turned to Italy—sideways a little, perhaps, that one eye might retain some scrutiny over the nominal gift of his Italian conquest to his mitred friend Adrian—thither hies Karl to settle this internal dissension among the Saracens. Short and sharp the conflict, and Karl comes back covered with the glory of a magnanimous interference, and not lacking that of conquest as well, his kingdom being the larger by that tract of land adjacent to his own terri-tory called the Spanish March. As he flies back to the east to meet the Saxons, who in their ponderous way are making good the opportunity of his absence from home, he leaves part of his forces in the lurch. This detachment being caught by enemies in, to them, unfamiliar mountain passes, is easily subdued despite the magic horn of the too heroic Roland, who here spills out his blue blood in vain, and thereby creates a perennial fount of inspiration at which the poets and romancers of the Middle Ages fill their cups.

And now to the east and that unknown north toward which Karl ever looked with longing eyes. The languid south, the insignificant west, have small charms for his large ambition. Those dark German forests, filled with strange barbarian foes, worshipping in weird temples marvellous idols—those famed Northmen, already vikings, mariners, pirates—they are " foemen worthy of his steel." The Saxons proved so, for it took thirty odd years to conquer them. Indomitable ones ! pouring out of their black forests fresh supplies to fill in the broken lines at the frontiers ; fighting to the death ; beaten back into the forests. " Conquered," say Karl and his Franks, flying south to the Lombards or west to Aquitaine, to stop some revolt broken out there. " Not so," says the Saxon Phœnix, rising from its ashes as soon as the conqueror's back is turned, boldly crossing the frontier, savagely plundering and harassing by way of filling up the interval. And so it goes between the Franks and the Saxons for thirty years, until—the temple razed, the Irminsul taken, four thousand Saxons butchered like sheep in a pen in one day by way of example—might makes the right, and the Saxons surrender. These things put age and discretion into even barbarian hearts. What can they do else ? Voltaire says : " Their gods were destroyed, their priests murdered amid the ruins of their idols. The unhappy people were converted with sabre cuts, and lo ! they become Christians and—slaves !" As to the first item in Voltaire's sarcastic conclusion we know something about that sort of Christianity, and the less said of it the better. They were baptized, these Saxons, even Witikind himself—their second Arminius, according to Hallam—laying down his arms and suffering the rite. But we of to-day know how much these Saxons became slaves. We know how they spilled over, in that their first panic, by no means wholly into France; how they fled north to become vikings and pirates; how they fled west across the water, pushing the Britons aside, mixing with the Normans, to make the English of to-day. But doubtless the Kaiser Karl thought he had absorbed the barbarous Saxon into Christian Frank forever, setting the fashion for those unsuspected Saxons of to-day who follow so religiously his pious policy.

The Saxons being disposed of, the dark and terrible Huns come next, remnants of Attila's Avars, swarming in from the east, centuries before. Into their dense jungles must this restless monarch next plunge, and with his usual fortune. Their settlements—called rings, circular inclosures of wooden buildings—are invaded and destroyed. And, true to his gospel, Karl gives them peace and goodwill by the sacrifice of their idols and temples, and the substitution of his own. Their national idol was a naked sword, symbolic of their deity, the sword-god; this these terrible Huns of Attila, now cowed and craven, must break in the presence of their conqueror, and they must come thereafter to the holy baptism of the Christians!

Surely a wonderful vitality somewhere is in this baptism! Three centuries before, it was a sight to remember when Clovis, with his Franks, bowed in the Cathedral of Rheims before the cross they had but lately burnt, and received the name of Christian. Then we beheld infant France before its sponsor, Rome. Now here stands our Christian Karl, himself sponsor to this Saxon leader Witikind, signing these fair-haired Saxons—these dark-browed Huns—with the sign of the cross, dropping upon each Christian baptism !

We have noticed that this great Karl ran down to Rome to visit his friend Hadrian, while his Franks were standing with drawn swords before Pavia. And Karl got quite in the way of running to Rome, until finally he made a most notable visit there, which must be enrolled also among his notable deeds ; for premeditated deed undoubtedly it was of Karl's, though coming about apparently as the pleasantest surprise. In the year 800 this visit took place. Four odd centuries since the sack of Rome by Alaric the Goth. Three odd centuries since Clovis set up the new Empire of France, and swelled with exultation over Roman plaudits in the streets of Tours. Christmas day in the year 800 was a day momentous to the ages ; a day of wedding and of funeral—wedding of one named Italy to one called France ; burial of one named Rome, finally and forever. And priest for both is Charlemagne, his head anointed with the royal unction, his person clad in the imperial purple, while Leo crowns, and all the Romans shout, " Long life to Charles ! Most pious Augustus ! crowned, by the grace of God, the great and pacific Emperor of the Romans !"

This was one of the deeds of Karl, and rather the most notable thing a man has achieved or can achieve ; enough to raise the ghost of Julius Cæsar from the purple dust it lay in. For in this ceremony the seal was set upon the political power of Rome. The old order vanished and gave place to new. Henceforth in place of Cæsars, popes

shall represent the Deity, and priests crowd out patricians.
Here, then, is Carolus Magnus, in the year 800 of our
Lord, Emperor of France, Germany, Italy, and Hungary —
and all this is *France !*—made from a strip of Rhine river
bank and five thousand barbarians led by Clovis into Gaul,
in the fifth century of our era ; there to stop and rest three
hundred years ; then to swell and swiftly break over every
boundary on east, and west, and north, and south, because of
Karl, the son of the mayor, a man too big for Gaul ; and so to
grow into that tremendous kingdom which included what
to-day is. Prussia, save a bit east of the Vistula, perhaps ;
Austria this western side the Danube ; and all between this
river line and the Ebro.

"No Pyrenees" then, O *grand monarque*, though your
grandson failed to hew them down ! No Rhine river
then, O Kaiser Wilhelm, though your Prussia lies one
side to-day ! That was a kingdom worth Napoleon's
dreams. France ! the centre of the world, the focus of
all brightness in those dusky times of the west. Rome
came to school to Paris then, and even haughty literary
Bagdad acknowledged its acquaintance. Constantinople,
too, shook hands with Karl, but warily, and taught a significant motto to its people, which ran thus : " Be friends
with the Franks, but be not neighbors !"

III.

We have, by this time, a hint of what Karl did in the
line of conquest. But other deeds remain whose color
is not red. Go to the secretary and hear him tell of

Karl's minsters, and his monasteries, and his schools ; of the masters he imported. Look at his laws, those famous Capitularies. Of them Montesquieu says, in his "Esprit des Lois :" "In Charlemagne's laws we see a vision which commands the view of all, and a wisdom which provides for all. . . . The father of a family could learn from him rules for the regulation of his household. . . . He arranged for the sale of the eggs from his farm—the same prince who divided among his people the incalculable treasure of the Huns who had plundered the world."

Of Charlemagne's learning we have spoken. Its limit seems to have been in the exhaustion of means of learning, and not at all in himself. His worshippers claim for him varied and voluminous authorship as well. Of this we have our doubts, though why Karl should not have "written" as well as wrought, we do not know. He was not the man to be behind the dead Cæsar, whose place he filled. If he wrote the epitaph upon Adrian's tomb he could certainly have written well, if at all. Wherever the merit of its literary composition lies, it is certain the sentiment it embodies was, as Gibbon observes, due the warm-hearted monarch. Here is a sample, which I translate from a German copy— Charlemagne's epitaph on the tomb of Adrian :

" Here I, Karl, engrave, while tears are swiftly thronging,
    Thy epitaph, O sweetest heart, father for whom I weep !
  Linger in my thought, O friend, while memory quiets longing !
    Christ, the King of Heaven, henceforth forever thee shall keep.

          *   *   *   *   *   *   *
  " Here our names united shall find no separation.
    Karol, King—Hadrianus, Pope—but briefly called to part !
  Ye who weeping look hereon, offer this supplication,
    ' Merciful God, receive these two to Thine all-healing Heart !' "

Well, Carolus Magnus, Emperor of Franks and Romans, conqueror of Spain, Saxony, Hungary, Lombardy, etc., improver of the empire, founder of literature, architecture, science in Europe of the Middle Ages, finally encountered a greater king than himself, and with little parley surrendered unconditionally. He died, and his body was laid in one of his famous minsters, and over his tomb was built an arch upon which his likeness and an inscription were engraved. The inscription certifies : "Here lies the body of Karl, the great and right worthy emperor, the illustrious improver of the empire, who reigned forty-seven years long," etc. Then the secretary goes on naïvely to tell of the wonders which ensued. For three years after Karl's death there were marvellous signs in the heavens. For a long time there was a black spot upon the sun. All this is recorded with the same simplicity which characterizes the entire biography. No doubt it is fitting that the order of nature should be disturbed when *Le Roi est mort !*

It is dear to the historical heart to talk of the hour and the man, as making the most marvellous connection in the most marvellous manner. As if the hour was ever wanting to the man, or the man to the hour !

The hour had struck for Charlemagne, and Charlemagne appeared—appeared to do the duty of the hour, to weld out of conflicting races the integral nation, which should be the Joshua of the new civilization. On the south lay Rome, sick unto death, yet grasping, with what grasp remained to that moribund old age, for the empire. The world had too long obeyed her mandates to easily shake off the habit of obedience, and an echo of other days still whispered in her feebly-voiced exactions. The divine right of

Rome had grown to be a superstition with the world, and it needed a nerveful young master to rouse it from such a nightmare. On the west stood Spain, with her Saracens massed against Gibraltar, beaten back but not destroyed by the hammer of the first Karl, waiting, watching their chance to pounce upon these fair Franks, to transform monasteries into mosques, and chain the Koran to the altar where the Bible lay.

On the east the black forests cast shadows perilous to the empire of Clovis. Swarthy savages, thicker than the forest leaves, watched in their lair the moment of the spring, when they might offer to their sword-god the sweet sacrifice of Frankish blood. Had that moment come ere Karl came to match it, the new civilization must have been retarded by another Middle Ages. Swarming over on all sides, they would have pushed east and west, annihilating, like the deluge, every former thing.

Across the forests shone the diadem of Constantinople. Corrupted with all manner of alien blood, the Eastern Empire had small virtue to keep sweet the world. And from the sunrise land the domes of Bagdad sent a menacing gleam. Plenty of claimants for the place of Rome were watching and planning for their hour. Had now the Carlovingian first monarch been such as was the Merovingian last—had a weak and silly Childeric arisen to fill the place of Pepin Bref, it needs no prophet's eye to discern what must have been ; with warring competitors within and crowding combatants without, France must have yielded to their combined blows and sunk beneath them. And what then ?

The seers must tell what then : but it needs no seer to

tell what *not* then. Not in this ninth century of our Christian era, Lombardy alchemized into Italy and put beneath
the feet of a strong master, in whose veins flowed neither
the degenerate blood of Greece nor the diseased blood of
Rome ; not Cæsar stamped out of the politics of the world ;
Mahomet turned faceward to Bagdad ; Saxon exiled from
the mainland and sent flying across the British Channel, and
there, wedding with his conquerors, in due time producing
the English of to-day ; not Hun and Avar put in apprenticeship to the civilizer. All this, but for the monarch in
whom the man met and matched the hour, could not
have been. Setting aside all romance of the Kaiser Karl,
all story of paladins, Ogier or Roland, eschewing all lovely
legend, we may indorse, in sober light of historic verity,
what La Motte Fouqué says of Charlemagne : " In him
was new Europe for the first time *one*. . . . He is the
father and creator of the German era !"

We have taken a far from comprehensive view of the
life, private and public, of one of the most conspicuous
figures in human history. Of the times upon which this
life fell we have given but a hint. Curiosity concerning
Charlemagne will never die out, and in proportion as his
true figure emerges from the mass of exaggerating fiction
and idealization which has surrounded it, it will attract a
deeper and more genuine interest. Around him centres
whatever is vital or worthy in the darkest and most
chaotic epoch of modern times, and in him is illustrated, as
perhaps in no other individual man, gigantic opportunity
meeting gigantic ability to mould the character of his own
and succeeding ages.

The author of " Undine," whose skill has found no worthy

compeer in certain delicate analytics, save Hawthorne, says again : " Whoever comes to compare Karl with any other monarch must not forget that outer deeds and their consequences do not reveal the inner being nor the essence of individuality." This is true only because of the limitations of the observer, and not because the phenomena of deed and life, as revealed by authentic history, could not show, were the observer sufficiently skilled and sensitive, the source of both, and the essence of character.

For my own part, I perceive Charlemagne to be a man of genius, whose necessity it was to meddle with all things at hand, and to bring to hand things remote, and whose good gift it was to have such a position in the world as gave to this necessity the largest scope. It is good to look upon this joyous, mighty man ; good to view his life ; good to see him, struck with death, make the sign of the cross and commend his spirit to his Lord ; good to mark the ripples which his advent sent circling down the sea of time, and which widen forevermore.

THE MONASTERY

THE MONASTERY.

Society had two aristocracies in the Middle Ages : the one of the State, the other of the Church. The former took form and front in the institution of chivalry ; the latter in that of the monastery.

The haughty chevalier, with lofty helmet and waving plume, with broidered doublet and jewelled girdle, with graceful cloak and burnished armor ; mounted upon his plunging steed, richly trapped with costly harness, attended by obsequious squire and servile suite—here was our lord of society, the bulwark and ornament of the State.

The humble monk, with bowed head enveloped in sombre cowl, his scanty gown dyed and stiffened by reason of his abstinence from the sinful luxury of ablution ; his body girt with a heavy rope, by way of showing that the beast was well in hand ; his flesh gashed with self-inflicted wounds and creased with ponderous chains and iron collars, to further signify its subjection ; his feet bare and bleeding with the stones and briers of untrodden ways ; perched upon some all but inaccessible rock, or buried in some cave usurped from wild-beast owner, or wandering upon the burning sands of some desert—here was another and superior lord of society, the bulwark and ornament of the Church. To these monastic aristocrats even royalty itself bowed in lowliest deference. Gibbon says : " Prosperity and peace introduced the distinction of the vulgar and ascetic Christian."

In the mediæval estimate, the highest-born noble, so long as he lived in the world and was engaged in its affairs, was the inferior of the monk, who, however obscure of birth or low in poverty, by virtue of his secession from the ranks of humanity, and his renunciation of all human ties and property, was a member of a superior aristocracy. The monastery, with its primitive lowliness, reared a loftier head than did the feudal castle.

I.

A body of men or women, never men *and* women, congregated and segregated, bound together by voluntary obedience to a set of rules involving renunciation of the world, with all that intimates of sacrifice ; vowing to poverty and solitude their mortal allegiance ; subjecting themselves to the direst extremities of exposure, hunger, and fatigue ; inflicting upon themselves all but intolerable torture to flesh and nerve ; seeking to expiate former utterance by present speechlessness, former action by present lethargy ; striving toward actual paralysis of all faculties which can connect the individual with the society ; a shadow of a living being amid shadows—this was monkhood. A crowd of devotees, herded loosely but permanently together, was the embryo monastery.

Antony of Egypt, in the third century, is doubtless the founder of the Christian monastery. This man in early life abandoned family and home, property and all social ties,

and wandered away from the cities of the living into a city
of the dead, a region of tombs, a place of stone-covered
caves filled with bones and the dust of human skeletons.
In this sepulchral solitude he found a sphere congenial to
his penitential purpose, and here he served out his self-
appointed time of penance, wounding and torturing his
despised body that he might rescue his soul from its thral-
dom. At the termination of this ascetic novitiate, he
struck into the wilderness, a three-days' journey, halting at
an isolated rock which seemed suitably remote and barren,
and this he chose for his mortal residence and place of
purgatory. But his solitude was destined to be broken.
There were other men in Egypt, in those days, who were
bewildered and in despair, in doubt of present and future,
ready to practise any device by which to lose the sense of
impending doom, to flee present persecution, to secure
future salvation ; multitudes then, as now, ready to follow
if not to lead. When, therefore, it was known that
Antony, the man, the neighbor, the Egyptian, had conceived such a plan, there were plenty to rush headlong in
his footsteps ; and Antony, from being the hermit of the
rock, became the abbot of the plain ; and the sands of that
Libyan desert, in the third century, became, before the
dawn of the Middle Ages, the arena of the first Christian
monastery, ruins of which, according to Gibbon, may be
seen to this day.

Antony lived one hundred and five years, and in that
centuried lifetime he saw, as it has been the lot of few
pioneers to see, his theory and practice propagated to a
wonderful extent. Pachomius, his pupil and successor,
was superior over seven thousand monks. Athanasius

visited Antony, caught his spirit, and carried the plan of monastic life to yet imperial Rome, where it ran rapidly the race of being "first endured, then pitied, then embraced." Martin of Tours, the bishop and soldier of the Franks, propagated the monastic institution in Gaul, and two thousand monks followed his body to the tomb—that body which in dust and ashes was still so potent to work miracles. Thence the fire leaped across the waters, and the tiny island of Iona, that Ultima Thule of the western world, caught the holy flame, and reflected back to Cyprus in the east an incendiary ray. Thus east and west, north and south, the flames of monasticism flew. And at the threshold of the Middle Ages we find the ground furrowed and sown with the seeds of that stupendous growth which, in the shape of the monastery, was to ripen through the season of a thousand years, tares and wheat, wheat and tares, growing together to the harvest.

In the sixth century came Benedict the Italian to weed and cultivate the sprouting crop of Antony's sowing. The Egyptian recluse had flung the seed, with careless hand, hither and thither, without order or precision. Where it fell there it lodged, and everywhere it sprouted ; but in wild confusion. Everywhere was to be found the monastic spirit, the monastic profession, the monastic practice. Here, as always, was needed the perfecter of the plan, who must follow the pioneer.

We do not see in Antony any hint of a dream in his own mind that he was the originator of a spiritual aristocracy. He had in view the salvation of the individual merely, and that individual principally the individual Antony. He fled from the things of time and sense to save his own soul alive, and if the soul of his brother also, so much the better. But we have no justification in history for ascribing to him wider or more ambitious hopes.

At the epoch of the sixth century the times were no longer the times of Antony. Already the Bishop of Rome had become Pope, and the policy of propagation had set in, and was giving incipient direction to religious thought and activity. Antony stood alone; but in Benedict's day we see coalition; already all things are done as means to an end, and that end the salvation of the individual *with* the establishment of the Church of Rome, as *sine quâ non*.

Benedict was not more a monk than a missionary, and not so much either as a reformer. Dante gives him a high place in Paradise, and makes him

" . . . the largest and most luculent"

among the pearls which floated into sight and sound, as he inspected those ghostly circles. Benedict, like Antony, refused to grapple with the problem of being in the world yet not of it. At the age of fourteen the profligacy of Roman school-boys repelled him, and he fled from their company into the solitudes of nature. Here a monk gave him a dress of his order, and pointed out to him a cave in which to meditate and do penance, and here he lived three years, receiving his necessary food from the patron monk, who let it down to him in his cave by a cord. But, like Antony, he was not suffered to remain in his cave undisturbed. The shepherds of the region found him out, and the monks of the vicinity chose him for their abbot. The fact that, having placed him in this position, these monks endeavored to poison him thereupon, is a fact rich in commentary on the character that monkhood had already attained. Montalembert says ("Monks of the West"): "Benedict had the ordinary fate of great men and saints. The great number of conversions worked by the example and fame of his austerities awakened a homicidal envy against him." Yet Benedict lived and did his work—and a great work for those days. He formulated rules for the regulation of monastic life which became "eventually the rule of all western monachism." He grappled with a lingering paganism, and on the ruins of a temple to Apollo, still in the sixth century the centre of the devotions of a pagan peasantry, he founded his famous Monastery of Monte Cassino ; and here, standing and with arms outstretched in prayer, *in articulo mortis*, he died. From this epoch the monastery acquires organic solidity and definite dignity. In the great Benedictine order we find the beginnings of systematic devotion and the germ of a more intellectual life. Of the works of the Benedictines, Sir Walter Scott says they are "of general and permanent advantage to the world at large, showing that the revenues of the Benedictines were not always spent in self-indulgence, and that the members of that order did not uniformly slumber in sloth and indolence." "The order increased so rapidly that the Benedictines must be regarded as the main agents in the spread of Christianity, civilization, and learning in the west" (Chambers's Encyclopædia).

Here, then, we find the monastery full-grown. The monks are no longer hermits, but students and propagandists.

Did a man covet the career of the monk and the glory

of monastic life ? He must first totally surrender every
tie and renounce all. Then he must stand for several
days at the monastery door and receive the affronts of the
porter, by way of testing his ascetic fortitude. This pre-
liminary being satisfactorily passed, he is conducted into
the reception-room of the monastery, and some superior
monk initiates him into the rules of monastic life. Among
these is implicit obedience to his superior, which one of
the fathers calls the monk's first virtue. He is to shun
laughter, to hold no private property, to live sparely, to
exercise hospitality, and, above all, to be industrious. He
is given a long black gown, with a cowl or hood of the same,
and a scapulary. After a novitiate of one year he becomes,
by solemn ceremonies, a monk in full. His life is now
one of unvarying routine, tedious or the contrary, according
to the wealth or poverty of his own individuality, for this,
however suppressed, must follow him within his cloister,
whether he will or no. His conditions are now remarkably
ill-calculated to make his mind his kingdom, for it must be
in defiance of his vows, if he gets any intellectual stimulus. His obligation of eternal poverty prevents all acquisition. He can call nothing his own. Such expressions
were severely punished. The rule of Columbanus—who
came after Benedict—inflicted six lashes for any *lapsus
linguæ* in which the possessive pronoun "my" slipped out.

The vow of implicit obedience in its full performance
surrendered intellect and conscience at once into the hand
of the abbot. The same Columbanus, who was an Irish
monk and a fair competitor for honor with Benedict in
missionary zeal, lays down one of his rules thus : " Any
monk who signs not the spoon with which he eats with the

sign of the cross, or who strikes the table with his knife, or who coughs at the beginning of a psalm, shall receive six lashes." In Maitland's "Dark Ages" we have quoted an instance of a monk who, pronouncing the Latin verb *to teach*, *docēre*, was bidden by the Abbot to say *docĕre ;* the ignorant abbot was obeyed, and we do not learn that the monk had the contumacy of Galileo, or that he muttered any accented penult in an undertone. This obedient monk was Lanfranc, afterward Archbishop of Canterbury.

II.

When we come to consider the causes from which the monastery arose, we shall find that they are not the monopoly of the Middle Ages, nor the special property of Christianity. The monastic spirit is inherent in man, and has found rare and isolated development in every age. If asceticism be a disease, yet it must be ranked among those diseases the seeds of which are born with us, and are called, whether scientifically or not, natural diseases. If we grant that the monastery is a monstrosity, we must admit also that the monstrous is everywhere possible, and own, with Goethe, "that it is in her monstrosities that nature reveals to us her secrets."

The idea which lies at the bottom, as corner-stone of the monastery, may be developed, on occasion, from any individual of the race. There is the making of a monk in every man.

What, then, was the occasion from which, in the Middle

Ages, the monastic spirit found so gigantic and dispropor-
tioned a development as to make that time seem to have
almost the monopoly of the monastery ?

The occasion is on the surface. It is the Middle Ages
itself—*the times*. Given a man with scrofula in his blood,
and yet so arrange his environment that his tendencies may
find no occasion for development ; give him climate, occu-
pation, food—all that tends to suppression of the humor,
and it may never break out. He may never, except from
say so, know he has it. Let the opposite conditions be
provided ; let the occasion be offered, and he will soon
discover, by its dire development, the inherent poison in
his system. The scrofula of monasticism boiled in the blood
of mediæval men, and the times afforded just those conditions which most favored its outbreak.

The times ! Never were such times. Humanity poised,
as it were, between the receding old and the advancing
new. Babylon fallen, but the captivity not ended. The
world torn by two mighty winds from opposite quarters,
one bringing thunders of regeneration and lightnings of
regeneration from the west, the other emptying vials of
wrath from the long tyranny of cloud-hung, rain-curtained
east. It was the unsettling of all things. The fall of
Rome had filled the world with the fragments of shattered
things, the rising Germanic Empire had covered all with a
pall of blood. Pagan temples lay prostrate, but the débris
was not cleared away, and the Christian Basilica struggled
up slowly, wrapped in a mist of the legend and fable of the
old idolatries. In these times of confusion men stood confused. Their limbs trembled beneath them ; their hearts
throbbed with apprehension ; their intellects failed them ;

only the suffering, affrighted soul within them hungered and aspired toward salvation. It was a time of panic—a time for men to rush, blind with fear and faith, through any door swung open before them which promised escape. Here, then, was the moment for the monastery. Its door swung open before panic-pursued multitudes, and tides of humanity swept over its portal out of the world.

For the thing was to get out of the world before the world got out itself. It was everywhere believed that the end of the world was near. The Church fathers taught and preached it. It was looming up, ever coming, and coming soon. And the influence of this belief contributed largely to the success of monastic propagation. Gregory I., as late as the sixth century, wrote to Ethelred in Briton that the end of the world was coming. What could it signify, then, how things went on in a world which was about to burn up? Material interests and possessions slipped easily from the grasp when the end of all things was so near at hand.

The mediæval man was a simple creature compared to our complex modern. In that great twilight space, out of which at any moment was to burst the fires of the last conflagration, there stood to his conception two ideas, and only two of much importance—his Flesh and his Spirit. *My body* and *my soul*—these made up the mediæval *ego*. Very distinct and wholly antipodal ; the one from above, the other from beneath, and between these two a great gulf fixed. Even so large and tender a genius as Gregory Nazianzen expresses this sentiment constantly in his poems, notably in " Soul and Body," which is thus translated by Mrs. Browning. To his soul, he says :

" What wilt thou possess or be?
 Oh, my soul, I ask of thee.
 What of great or what of small
 Counted precious therewithal?
 Be it only rare and want it,
 I am ready, Soul, to grant it!

*　*　*　*　*　*

" . . . what wilt thou be,
 Oh, my soul? a deity?
 A god before the face of God,
 Standing glorious in His glories,
 Choral in His angels' chorus?

*　*　*　*　*　*

 " Go! upon thy wing arise.
 Pluméd by quick energies,
 Mount in circles up the skies;
 And I will bless thy wingéd passion,
 Help, with words, thine exaltation,
 And, like bird of rapid feather,
 Outlaunch thee, Soul, upon the ether."

But to the body, Gregory, the poet, speaks thus:

" But thou, O fleshly nature, say
 Thou with odors from the clay,
 Since thy presence I must have,
 As a lady with a slave.

*　*　*　*　*　*　*

 May some rocky house receive thee
 Self-roofed, to conceal thee chiefly!"

Then he goes on to show what this beast-body may claim
as its due—only so much as to keep it as a tenement of
spirit, alive, and with such necessaries promises it a rope
besides, calling it a household foe.

That subtle Briareus of science and sanity, the Intellect,

which in these days stands between flesh and spirit, and with a
hundred hands and voices entreats the one to be reconciled to
the other, was lacking then.   Men were Manichees, and believed their bodies to be wholly antagonistic to their spirits.
They believed, with intense conviction, that the soul was
worth saving, and could be saved only by crucifixion of the
flesh.   The body is beast possessed by devil, whose sole
function is to tempt and ruin.   The soul must be torn from
its enchanter, the evil wizard, flesh.   In these two ideas
lies the key to the gigantic monastery of the Middle Ages.

This simple man, made up of soul and body, was easily
persuaded.   He stood, like a child overtaken by a storm in
the forest, bewildered and frightened, and ready to follow
whithersoever led.   And his leaders led him into the monastery.   In the fourth century, Jerome, learned and wealthy,
the princely father of the Primitive Church, says of himself : " I voluntarily condemned myself to this prison and
exile for fear of hell, having no other company but scor-
pions and wild beasts. . . .   I often joined whole nights to
the days, crying, sighing, and beating my breast, . . . and,
being angry and armed with severity against myself, I went
alone into the most secret part of the wilderness, and if I discovered anywhere a deep valley or craggy rock, that was the
place of my prayer ; there I threw this miserable sack of my
body."   And he breaks out eloquently in praise of and persuasion to monastic life thus : " O desert, enamelled with
the flowers of Christ !   O solitude, where those stones are
built of which, in the Apocalypse, is built the city of
God !   O retreat, which rejoicest in the friendship of God !
What doest thou in the world, my brother, with thy soul
greater than the world ?   How long wilt thou remain in the

shadow of roofs, and in the smoky dungeons of cities ? Believe me, I see here more of the light." Indeed, Jerome was a prime propagator of monastic life at this early day. It was he who brought into the folds of the monastery the illustrious Roman widow Paula, with all her vast wealth, her daughters included. And she becomes straightway a heroine of the times and times after, Jerome eulogizing her thus : " If all the members of my body were changed into tongues—if all my limbs resounded with a human voice, yet should I be incapable of sounding her praises." Chrysostom, " who in his preaching so carried away his audiences that they beat the pavement with their swords and called him the thirteenth apostle," wrote and preached, with his surpassing enthusiasm and eloquence, of the monastic life as above all others. No other is comparable to it ; indeed, he intimates that no one outside of the monastery is quite certain of salvation. This teaching and persuasion continued all through the Middle Ages. In the twelfth century St. Bernard, called " Mellifluous Doctor," uses all his eloquence still in favor of monasticism. Vaughan, in his " Hours with the Mystics," says : " With Bernard the monastic life is the one thing needful. He began life by drawing after him into the convent all his kindred. . . . His incessant cry for Europe is, ' Better monasteries and more of them ! ' " Thus on all sides we find persuasion to the monastic life. No one was excluded ; the soldier might desert his standard, but if he deserted into the monastery he incurred no dishonor. It was to all classes an asylum, an alternative where alone could satisfaction be found. To those whose lives were well worn out in the pleasures and sins of the world it offered place for repentance. Pliny, as early as his day, describes

the monasteries he encounters in his travels as the abode of
" a solitary race, but constantly replenished by penitents
from the outer world." This before the thick darkness of
the Middle Ages had gathered. And when the darkness
had passed away, in the Elizabethan age, we find the great
Emperor Charles V. abdicating the crown of Germany and
Spain to enter a monastery. Of him Byron says :

> " The Spaniard, when the lust of sway
>   Had lost its quickening spell,
> Cast crowns for rosaries away,
>   An empire for a cell."
>
> —*Ode to Napoleon.*

To the abjectly poor it offered betterment in temporal
affairs. None so low in life but he might rise to distinction here, had he the fortitude to exceed others in
austerity. A poor shepherd might make himself immortal
as Charlemagne if he had invention and endurance in
making himself miserable. Such an one was Simeon, the
ingenious Syrian shepherd, who deserted his sheep and
built himself a pillar of stones, gradually reaching the
height of sixty feet. Here he skilfully balanced himself
thirty years. Gibbon says : " Successive crowds of pilgrims
from Gaul and India saluted the divine pillar of Simeon."
He was all but adored by kings and queens. The Emperor
Theodosius consulted him on affairs of Church and State ;
his funeral was royal in its pageantry. Indeed, there was
scarcely a passion of human nature to which the monastery
could not appeal to win recruits. All that could soothe
conscience, all that could flatter vanity, all that could
promise humility, all that could tempt ambition, had here

a settled residence. There is indeed plenty of reason for
the existence of the monastery, and its gigantic proportion
in the Middle Age is less and less mysterious the more we
look into that age. Nor must we go too far in condemna-
tion of those, the holy fathers of the Christian faith, who,
in the midst of a crooked and perverse generation, contributed so largely to the excessive growth of monastic life.
Rather let us attain to the temper of Charles Kingsley, and
seek to find, as he says, " some apology for the failings of
such truly great men as Dunstan, Becket, and Dominic,
and of many more whom, if we hate, we shall never understand, while we shall be but too likely, in our own way, to
copy them." Kingsley says, in his preface to the " Saint's
Tragedy " : " The Middle Age was, in the gross, a coarse,
barbarous, and profligate age. . . . It was, in fact, the very
ferocity and foulness of the times which, by a natural revul-
sion, called forth at the same time the apostolic holiness and
the Manichean asceticism of the mediæval saints. The
world was so bad that to be saints at all they were compelled
to go out of the world. . . . But really time enough has
been lost in ignorant abuse of that period, and time enough
also, lately, in blind adoration of it. When shall we learn
to see it as it was, the dawning manhood of Europe, rich
with all the tenderness, the simplicity, the enthusiasm of
youth, but also darkened, alas ! with its full share of youth's
precipitance and extravagance, fierce passions, and blind
self-will ; its virtues and its vices colossal, and for that very
reason always haunted by the twin-imp of the colossal--the
caricatured."

III.

What other than a calamity could that be considered which took away from both Church and State its best and purest-minded citizens ?   Yet this was precisely the immediate effect of the monastery upon its own times.   Thousands upon thousands from those mediæval societies, so needing manhood and Christianhood, were swept by this monstrous epidemic superstition.   In Egypt, in the century in which Antony lived, it is stated that the number of citizens thus nullified to the state was equal to those left. Centuries before the feudal system settled like the stone of a sepulchre upon the masses entombed beneath it—centuries before chivalry issued in its haughty aristocracy therefrom, did the monastery draw to its silent prison the men and women in whom, save for this curdling superstition, was virtue enough to keep the whole world sweet.   In vain did the emperors issue decrees against this decimation of the State.   The eloquence of the fathers, the tyranny of diseased conscience, exceeded in authority the mandates of the Cæsars.

In the beginning it is the individual who must be saved at price of all penance and renunciation.   In the end it is the Church that must prosper at the cost of all individual character—the individual contributing to the prosperity of the Church will be saved as a matter of course.   In the beginning the monastery is a hermit, then a company of monks—cenobites having all things in common—living on rocks, in caves, subsisting on air and prayer.   In the end it is the gorgeous monastery of elaborate architecture—the mitred abbot with retinue like a king, with royal refectory, with feudal acres, lord over a spiritual aristocracy.

All along the line, however, we see effort at reform and restoration of the early ideal. After Antony, with a lapse of four odd centuries, comes Benedict, to put in order and subject to rule ; after Benedict, by six odd centuries, come Francis and Dominic, to engraft the early good fruit on the aging, corrupt tree ; and again, in the fourteenth century, we see the Augustinian reformer. Yet this was the order in which, in the sixteenth century, Luther found the need and the germ of a more radical and permanent reformation. And Luther stands to us in total contrast to any ideal, early or late, of monastic life. Pre-eminently a man among men, most human in humanity, we see in his character, and his creed, and his work the eternal antagonism of Christianity to monachism.

To its own times, then, we must view the institution of monastic life as containing more the constituents of a curse than a blessing. But he who comes to bring this indictment must not sum up his case before he has studied the effect of the monastery on succeeding times. And with a lengthening sweep of vision we may discern results from this institution on succeeding ages which, to both State and Church—to society and Christianity rather—have been untold blessings.

Society owes to the monastery its democracy. This offshoot from mediæval society preserved in its aristocracy of asceticism the individual to the State. Feudal aristocracy took all the men and women, in Lady Montagu's use of that phrase. They alone came to the surface ; there was no chance for the low-born and the underling. Mind was no measure of the man in those days—would never have been, save for the gradual development of the intellectual through the narrow but deep channels of the scholasticism of the monasteries. Here the *vulgus* could rush in and compel recognition and deference. Gregory VII., the gigantic constructive genius of the Middle Age, the son of a carpenter, could work his way through the cell of the monk to the papal chair, and there compel homage and submission from an emperor. The Church of the Middle Ages recognized always the individual, and the coarsest and poorest might be transmuted into fine gold through the crucibles of cloister and cell. This bare suggestion may be developed with logical sequences until we realize the grand causality of this institution of mediæval times, in the evolution of a true democracy of modern times.

To the evolution of a practical Christianity in succeeding times the monastery brings also an incalculable factor. Ideals in manhood and Christianhood emerge into view, by successive action and reaction. Doubtless the world must some time have tried the monastic ideal. The egregious mistake that it is clearly seen to be with the vision that comes after the event, could never have been so seen before the event. St. Jerome would not advise the monastic life in the days of Kingsley and Stanley ; yet how can we be sure that a Kingsley or a Stanley would not have erred with St. Jerome in his own day ? Certain it is that the problem how to live in the world but not of the world still confronts those who would be unworldly ; and as certain that Christendom has, once for all, had it proven that the problem is not solved by isolation from the world.

And yet it could ill afford to spare these pioneer monks,

who, with all their excesses and painful perversions, are
" those without whom we could not be made perfect."
Montalembert says : " Who has not contemplated, if not
with the eyes of faith, at least with the admiration inspired
by uncontrollable greatness of soul, the struggles of these
athletes of penitence ? . . . Everything is to be found there
—variety, pathos, the sublime and simple epic of a race of
men earnest as children and strong as giants."

One great common benefit to both mediæval and modern
world the monastery subserved—a benefit so transcendent
that for it we forgive all its egregious suicide of citizen and
Christian, its incarceration and mutilation of each. It did
for us what could have been done by no other means in this
ruined and ruinous epoch of time—it kept us our books.
The storm raged everywhere, but here was safe repository,
and in the advanced years of the monastic institution the
compilation and copying of these priceless manuscripts was a
leading feature of the industrious life of a monk. The
Scriptorium of the monastery is to us moderns hallowed
ground, and for it we may forget its cells and their terrors.

The monastery of the Middle Ages has passed away with
the times that gave it birth. In place of a squalid encamp-
ment spread upon the burning sands of Africa, sentineled
with hermit huts, a circle of separate cells where ascetics of
superior piety burrowed like moles in the sand—in place of
the rocky rendezvous of northern lands, swarming with its
busy brotherhood—in place of the opulent abbey, where
sensual abbot and worldly friar in a later day became the
minions of popes and the masters of men—in place of all
this we have, here and there, a lichened abbey, a vacant
pile of mediæval architecture, in Africa, in Palestine, in

Italy, whose crumbling ruins make a melancholy monument
to the fanatic populace that once thronged their cells and
now lie in the dust beneath them.   Here and there, indeed,
the traveller finds a roof and shelter, food and lodging, a
lighted fire and a kindly welcome from the modern friar,
whose length of belt and ringing laugh tell no tale of early
days.   Rarely, indeed, as at La Trappe, may the ghost of
Antony be fancied to revisit his degenerate progeny, degenerate even in the austere rule and miserable asceticism of
the terrible Trappists.   As we gaze upon the ruins of the
mediæval monastery, and as our imagination summons before
us from their dust a multitude of mediæval monks and nuns,
led by the saintly Antony, who bends beneath the hundred
years of his tortured existence ; a courtly Basil, eloquent
and learned ; a Roman matron, Paula, in whose veins were
mingled blood of Grecian Agamemnon and Roman Grac-
chus, whose wealth embraced a city of Augustinian grandeur ; a shepherd, Simeon, self-chained to his pillar's summit through the fires of thirty summers, through the frosts
of thirty winters, bending in the blast beneath the sun, beneath the stars, with ceaseless wail for " mercy, mercy !"—
when we mark the myriads that follow in their wake, noble
with peasant, scholar with clown, all alike with bowed
head, and downcast eye, and emaciated figure, loaded with
iron greaves and collars, covered with hair like the beasts
among whom they lived, winding in and out of narrow,
vacant, unlit cells, bending before the cross which everywhere confronts them—when we hear their wailing Miserere
echoing through the silent air, when we behold their pain-
sharpened features, their sunken eyes glowing with terror of
remorse, pleading for absolution, their ghastly glances fixed

upon an approaching doom which diseased conscience peoples with demon and avenger—alas ! what spectacle has history presented that equals this for melancholy ?

The mediæval monastery has passed away. It will not return. But *monachism* remains, and will remain while human nature bides its time. Over and over again will a wretched phantasy of conscience bid the conscience-stricken turn his back on homely, present duty in the battle-plain of life, and make the same old experiment of self-salvation in unhallowed renunciations. The spirit of Monachism has survived the mediæval monastery. Its profitless experiments, its unavailing renunciations, are not now confined to convent walls. Not among those luminous figures which emerge from the modern convent to carry the comfort of the Cross to battle-field and prison-cell and hospital cot, do we find the painfulest examples of its sad misleading ; but in the selfish segregations of the fashionable cliques, the complacent hypocrisy of social ostracisms, of scientific unbelief, of sated, soulless culture, of morbid research, of wretched introspection, of indolent abstraction from the practicabilities of life. The mediæval man fled into the monastery ; the modern man flees into himself, and all unconsciously, in manifold ways, repeats the old vain folly of a selfish subjectivity.

Hundreds of years before Antony of Egypt laid the corner-stone of the mediæval monastery a young man sat on an Eastern throne, ruler over countless myriads of servile subjects, owner of all the wealth of India. Yet, though swaying so potent a sceptre, seated on so towering a throne, wearing so glittering a crown, the soul within this youthful monarch tortured him to a strange sacrifice for its sake.

He abandons all—throne, subjects, wealth, pleasure, power
—and, searching out the meanest and most abject slave in
his realm, takes from him his tattered, filthy robe, and puts it
on his own royal form, and thus disguised goes forth from
all humanity to be alone.   In trackless forest and in barren
desert, in cave of beast and rock of eagle, he serves out his
self-appointed term of penance and probation ; and when
this is accomplished he returns, another being from another
world, and lays before his subjects, among whom is none
so poor as he, the true wealth he has found—the secret of
existence, the *summum bonum* of human life, the knowledge how to lose existence, how to submerge human life,
how to annihilate the individual.

Behold in Buddhism the genius of the monastery !   Behold in Gautama the prototype of Antony !

But midway between Antony and Gautama behold the
Nazarene, the young Carpenter, the Evangelist, the Son,
the Brother, the Man of Bethlehem—behold Him entering
into all the joys and sorrows of the manhood which He
dignified, wearing graciously to its last humiliation the garb
of human flesh to which He has ever joined in honorable
wedlock the unassailable human soul—behold Him, from
His manger-cradle to His death-bed cross, pre-eminently
the Man of men, fullest of humanity, whose whole burden
of mission to us lies epitomized in His own statement : " I
am come that ye might have life, and that ye might have it
more abundantly."

Life !   Life !   A more intense, individual human life !

> " 'Tis life of which our views are scant—
> More life, and fuller, that we want !"

The humanity of each of us is like some Æolian harp

constructed by the Master Musician and laid down tenderly by Him upon the sea-shore where winds from every quarter play continuously. Buddhism would sweep into the vast ocean this palpitating lyre, and mix its several elements indistinguishably in the deep waters. Mediæval monasticism would heap it with sand and bury its melodies from every human ear. An enlightened Christianity would leave it, free and sensitive, upon the shore—would open it to all the winds that hurry to and fro, that it may give out to heaven and earth its full completed harmony.

Behold in Christianity the antipode of Buddhism, the antidote of Monachism!

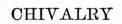

CHIVALRY

CHIVALRY.

As the word Chivalry falls upon our ears a motley multitude, in shadowy panorama, glides before us. Here gleam
the lances of a Richard, lion-hearted, a Godfrey, a Ray-
mond, a St. Louis ; blending anon with cross and staff of
barefooted pilgrim, or hermit Peter, or pauper Walter, *sans
savoir*, or priestly St. Bernard ; changing with ample turban of remorseless Turk and flashing cimetar of bearded
Saracen, worn and borne by a Suleiman or a Saladin.   Or
perhaps we think of an Arthur or a Tancred, summing up
in one the virtues of the ideal knight,

> " Who reverenced his conscience as his king,
> Whose glory was redressing human wrongs,
> Who spake no slander, no, nor listened to it,
> Who loved one only, and who clave to her."

This masculine perfection is broad and tall, a splendid
giant, mounted always on a plunging charger, with drawn
lance and tossing plume, with broidered doublet and
jewelled girdle beneath the graceful cloak which hangs
with careful carelessness on the left shoulder.   This, if our
author chance to be Tasso, or Tennyson, or Sir Walter
Scott.

If, however, we have fallen upon Cervantes and gained
from him our notion of the mediæval chevalier, straightway
the name evokes the Knight of the Sorrowful Figure, with

disjointed, rattling armor, mounted on his wind-broken
steed, with pasteboard vizor, making furious raids on wind-
mills, attended at a comfortable interval by his somnolent,
sententious squire solidly astride a stiff-legged ass !—the
one sublime, the other ridiculous, and both fictions. Yet,
if there be but one step from the sublime to the ridiculous,
that step must be our *via media;* and here, if anywhere
between the two extremes, shall we find our veritable historic chevalier.

We cannot deny that inclination might turn us to one
side alone and leave us there, were inclination not in league
with conscience in this research. We would rather believe
in the exquisite Tancred of Tasso, the impassioned Orlando
of Ariosto, with their superhuman virtues and valors, their
transcendent prowess and fortitude, than in something less.
But we must take what history gives us.

I.

In our brief study of mediæval chivalry we must hold
ourselves ready at any time to separate the spirit of chivalry
from the institution of chivalry, to which it gave rise.

The spirit of chivalry may be inferred from the vow
which in its early history was confession of faith to the
chevalier, and is thus epitomized : " To speak the truth, to
succor the helpless and oppressed, and never to turn back
from an enemy." Fidelity, clemency, courage, courtesy—
these four seem to sum up the main points of the chivalric
code. From this vow, taken by youths of noble lineage at

the age of twenty-one, and accompanied with the investiture
of arms, arose the institution of chivalry, which, from small
to large, grew, in the lapse of time, into the vast proportions
of a military organization, and for several centuries formed
a cavalry which was the nearest approach to and substitute
for a standing army in the new nations of Europe.

The ceremony of initiation into the rank of chevalier at
the age of twenty-one was preceded by a regular education
from the age of seven. From this time up to the age of
fourteen the boy was page to the lords and ladies in the
castle of his feudal superior, and at this impressible age
acquired, from association with its votaries, the notions and
manners of chivalry. The next seven years he was called
squire, and his duties were those of attendance upon his
superior at tournament, or joust, or real battle, where skill
and prowess in the field duties of knighthood were acquired.
Then, this seven years of apprenticeship being served, at
the age of twenty-one the young squire takes the vow pre-
scribed, is invested with arms, and made a knight in the
presence of an assembled multitude.

Command imagination to present you at this scene. Let
us join this multitude of fair women and brave men over
whom the sun, reflected from myriad glittering lances,
sheds a dazzling light. Behold in the centre of this arena,
to which all eyes are turned, the young Frank, massive of
form, fair of face, lofty of mien. Listen, while every ear
is strained and every sound is hushed, as with ringing voice
he vows toward Heaven to "speak the truth, to succor the
helpless and oppressed, and never to turn back from an
enemy." Behold him now kneel as his sovereign lord
invests him with the belt and spurs, and places in his hand

the lance of chivalry, while with his own he strikes the glowing cheek of the young chevalier one blow as token of the last insult he shall endure.

II.

There has been much dispute and research as to when chivalry was instituted. Hallam says " chivalry may, in a general sense, be referred to the age of Charlemagne." In the Cabalarii of Karl we find the equipment and investiture of the cavalier, if not his creed and conduct. These pet soldiers were matched by the Milites of the eleventh and twelfth centuries, when feudalism had established aristocracy among the nations of Europe. In the decentralization of sovereign power which followed the taking off of Charlemagne, there began to be many centres of government and society, inside circles, and wheels within wheels. The king stood, with his dukes, at the centre of the system. Barons circled outside and revolved about these, themselves being centres of still outer circles, composed, in turn, of their subordinates, who were sometimes nobles, but inferior; sometimes free men, but dependent; sometimes serfs, who were to their lords little more than chattel property.

This state of society reached its worst and best in the period between the ninth and twelfth centuries. The anarchy which ensued in the kingdom of France upon the death of Charlemagne, the extinction of the Carlovingian and the usurpation of the Capetian dynasty, may be regarded as parent occasion to the development of that subsequent aristocracy of which the head and front is found in the institution of chivalry. From out the ranks of this feudal aristocracy could be summoned, on occasion, an armed and mounted cavalry to serve in its defence ; and the relation of vassal and superior was, in its origin, not inimical to the development of many of the virtues and graces of chivalry.

The question, Where was chivalry born ? may be answered in a monosyllable. For in that twilight time the stars shone chiefly on one spot. Not Italy, decrepit and dismembered ; not Germany, the prey of savages from eastern wilds ; not Spain, as yet unallied with Germany and standing, quite at bay, with lance of French hunter on the east, and howl of wolfish Moslem on the west ; not England, unarisen from the ground where Saxon grapples Norman ere their wrestle grows to an embrace.

Nowhere but over France is there space of tranquil sky in which the star of chivalry can rise and reach its zenith. And there it burns, illuminating the neighboring nations, and lighting distant ones with a lengthened ray. The fiery Spaniard, senile Roman, sullen Saxon, and afar the subtle Saracen copy the graces of the chevalier of France, despite the intermittent discords among their nationalities. The ferocity of their wars is greatly mitigated by the manners and virtues of the code of chivalry. The chronic quarrels between the Capetians and Plantagenets were less brutal than any battles ever were. Hallam says : " In the wars of Edward III., originating in no real animosity, the spirit of honorable as well as courteous conduct toward the foe seemed to have arrived at its highest point." Ruskin says : " The

battle of Agincourt is romantic, and of Bannockburn, simply because there was an extraordinary display of human
virtue in both these battles." There was much of the joust
and something of the tournament in these engagements, despite the bloodshed. In the closing decade of the eleventh
century the star of chivalry rested in its zenith over the
sepulchre in Palestine, and was reflected thence until all these
tilting lancers—Spaniard, Saxon, German, and Italian—
rallied round the chevalier of France, and bore in common
cause a common lance beneath the Oriflamme !

We gaze upon this phenomenon of chivalry, pre-eminent
not only in the history of society in the Middle Ages, but
pre-eminent in the history of society in all ages, and we
wonder whence this wondrous bloom amid the desert. We
look so unbelievingly upon the good side of our humanity
that a development there is first incredible and then unaccountable. A Sardanapalus does not tax our credulity, nor
a Nero—the horrors of ancient and modern pagan societies ;
but a Gautama, a Socrates, an Aurelius upon the throne of
the Cæsars, an Epictetus in the days of Nero—these strain
our credulity, and we constantly wonder how it was. Yet in
my view it is to the unadulterated good in humanity that we
must refer the rise and development of this pre-eminent
phenomenon of chivalry. It is true these knights had
the historic Christ, and some of them loved and served
Him with the knightly love that makes all who have it
" Knights of the Holy Ghost ;" for the modern phenomenon, a Christian, has in him the mediæval phenomenon,
a chevalier. But the institution of chivalry did not spring
from Christianity, nor were the creed, tradition, or practice
of what the theologians call revealed religion any essential

of the creed, tradition, or practice of chivalry ; yet it had its springs in the religious nature of man ; it sprang from the necessity of man to create for himself an ideal, from that inalienable endowment of human nature by which we must worship, aspire, obey.

This position takes very general ground, and does not prevent the entrance of many particulars which may fill the interval lying between first cause and effect. Thus some say the seeds of the Socratic teachings, the Stoic philosophies, or that of Boethius, nearer their own times, put the thought of chivalry into these mediævals, and caused the formulation of its sublimely simple creed. This may be or may not be ; I only claim for these mediæval men that they could have thought this thought unassisted.

Speaking of links in the chain of causation, however, I must mention one which was certainly original with these mediævals—the *woman* in it ! The romancers and poets, Chaucer at their head, make her the first cause here ; this I do not admit ; but I shall do no violence to my convictions if I consent to call this natural religion, which was not the worshipping, obeying, and following of a historic Christ, the worshipping at least of woman. And here we strike upon the great distinguishing characteristic of chivalry— something we find nowhere else—its mystic ideal, the woman. The last lines of Goethe's greatest work sums up the essence of the chevalier's theology : " Ever the woman-soul leadeth us on." The *Ewigweibliche* was their misty, mystic deity ; the woman supplied to them their anthropomorphic deity. Of course what I have said by way of indicating the line of thought along which we must travel in order to arrive at the parent causes of chivalry relates to the spirit or theory of chivalry rather than to the institution.   I suppose we need not search long for the causes of Charlemagne's Cabalarii.   The idea in the busy brain of the monarch which brought about the organization of this fine cavalry was not more religious, I presume, than that which produced the Tall Regiment of Frederick William of Prussia, or the invincible Beef-Eaters of Henry VII. and Victoria of England.   Cause here is resolved into occasion, and both are on the surface.

The institution of chivalry, as it became elaborated and corrupted with accretions alien to its spirit, lost its chemistry, and became a thing of mechanism.   Its affinities unlocked, and its substance went into solution.   From this solution came, as permanent political precipitate, the standing armies of Europe.   Its fantastic adornments and sentimental practices passed, as its superficial social crystal, into the courtiers of later days, the cavaliers of English Stuart and French Bourbon *régimes*.   That intrinsic, indestructible, immutable element, the spirit of chivalry, evaporated into those high regions whence it came and comes again, wooing, by its gentle virtues, from the soil of all ages rare blooms of knightly service to the world.

Hallam says the invention of gunpowder made an end of the institution of chivalry.   This engine of modern civilization was known in the thirteenth century, but did not reach efficiency in warfare until the commencement of the fifteenth.   The Crusades of the twelfth and thirteenth centuries engrafted upon chivalry that excessive elaboration which is the inevitable precursor of corruption in all human institutions.   In time the golden article of chivalry—clemency to the weak and conquered, and courtesy to all—took

on the character of gallantry toward women, which was, as
its workings show, either a sensual sophistry or a fantastic
sentimentality, emasculating ideal knighthood. I think, in
a sense not wholly literal, Hallam is right. The cannon of
the fifteenth century blew up the thing still bearing the
name of chivalry. The gun superseded the lance. The
pomp and circumstance of chivalry dispersed, its day being
done. But when the artillery of modern times levelled this
breastwork of the mediævals, if fallen, as a whole, there yet
remained fractions of the structure, but units in themselves,
imperishable granite stones wedged into the edifice which
no shock could disintegrate, and which will endure, for the
admiration of the ages. There were immortal lords and
ladies—for, as we have seen, ladies were *sine quâ non*
of knights—men and women—*the* men and women—the
world's best—aristocracy of all the ages—a Spanish Cid,
" inferior to none that ever lived in frankness, honor, and
magnanimity," Hallam says ; and Schlegel calls him an
ineffaceable picture " of the single-minded and true-hearted
old Castilian spirit, . . . undoubtedly the genuine history"
of the man—true Spanish gold in exchange for all Quixote
counterfeits ; and the Donna Ximena, his wife, full in-
demnity for all Dulcineas ; a Richard, lion-hearted and yet
shedding knightly tears of knightlier penitence at his father's
grave—solid gain for any dubious, superhuman Arthur ; a
veritable Tancred in good change for Tasso's saint ; and his
uncle, Robert Guiscard, the Norman knight of marvellous
renown, whom Gibbon describes as " of lofty stature, surpassing the tallest of his army ; his complexion ruddy, his
shoulders broad, his hair and beard long and of flaxen
color, his eyes sparkling with fire, while his voice, like that

of Achilles, could impress obedience and terror amid the
tumult of battle—wielding his sword in one hand, in the
other his lance, thrice unhorsed in battle of which he was
most eminent victor over eminent victors.'' Of less fleshly
splendor is a St. Louis, most tender son, most valiant Christian, whose virtues and graces realize the Arthur of poetry ;
and his mother, Regent Blanche, every inch a monarch and
every inch a mother ; and his seneschal, the Sieur de Join-
ville, of frankest heart, most lovable in child-like chivalry.

Some antiquarians seem afraid of too much light upon
these fine antiques, and perhaps many of us may have a
subtle suspicion that by a too free ventilation these time-
tinted portraits may lose those lovely hues of age which
suffice to stamp them as '' genuine.'' This feeling comes
from the enchantment which distance lends to our ideals,
and is something to be gently criticised. But in this particular case I think there is small ground for fear. Rob
him of much with which hero-worship invests him, and there
still remains to this mediæval chevalier that which will ever-
more preserve and distinguish him. One or two of his
characteristics are lost to us moderns, and will forever stamp
him *sui generis*. There are and will be men as strong of
heart, but there never will or can be, I venture, men so
strong of nerve and muscle—men of such physical perfections, of such matchless prowess, of such superb endurance.
We need not go far to find causes for our degeneration from
this stature of the perfect physical man, and we need not
take space to apologize for it ; it remains a fact, and one
upon which we shall not try to congratulate ourselves. Those
mediæval knights are men to look at with a sigh. Men de-
void of aches, and pains, and dyspepsias ; men without

nervous headaches ; men to whom coddling and " soothing" were not indispensable.   Alas ! there are no duplicates of this picture among the men of our day ; and the negative was not preserved.

Then there is a quality of mind to match this physical attribute which cannot be restored by any modern process— the quality of *unconsciousness of self ;* lack of that essential ubiquity, self, which our refinements of analysis and vivisection have fastened, like an " eating lichen," to the thought of all thinkers ; that critical detective which unceasingly attends our footsteps, never letting down his watch. The places that we moderns tread are vastly finer than those barren rooms of the mediævals.   Our feet sink deep in soft Axminster, and our spacious parlors are crowded with every possible and impossible appointment for use, and luxury, and enervation.   We look down upon the owners of those rude oak-raftered halls, wherein was only board and bench. But our magnificent apartments are everywhere hung with mirrors.   Every article is a reflector, and nowhere can the opulent occupant look that he can fail to see his own image. We are ever in the custody of self-officered police, and cannot forget ourselves long enough to breathe freely. They—the mediævals, the unencumbered—they were free ! strong, simple-minded children, unspoiled by " notice." A Dr. Samuel Johnson would have been an impossibility among these open-air men of deeds ; but could he have existed, he could never, in those times, have had his Boswell !

Nay, take this mediæval knight, with his physical perfections, his unconsciousness of self, his picturesque costume, his gentle mien, his powerful carriage, his knightly courtesy, " expressing," says Hallam, " the most highly refined

good breeding, founded less on the knowledge of ceremoni-
ous politeness—though that was not to be omitted—than on
the spontaneous modesty and self-denial and respect for
others which ought to spring from the heart;" with that
inviolable faith toward all, which made of every knight a
Regulus, and we have a picture of a man of such proportions that, "taken for all in all, we ne'er shall look upon
his like again." Something better we shall see and do see,
yet not the same. "Never, never more," says Burke,
"shall we behold that generous loyalty to rank and sex,
that proud submission, that dignified obedience, that subor-
dination of heart which kept alive, even in servitude itself,
the spirit of an exalted freedom; . . . that sensibility of
principle, that chastity of honor which felt a stain like a
wound, which inspired courage while it mitigated ferocity,
which ennobled whatever it touched. . . . Chivalry, the
unbought grace of life, the cheap defence of nations, the
nurse of manly sentiment and heroic enterprise!"

III.

And now the childish treble of that ubiquitous little
Peterkin, the *enfant terrible* to historians, breaks in with
the question, sometimes so embarrassing to us Kaspars,

> "But what good came of it?"

The benefits which such an institution, founded upon
such principles, must necessarily have conferred upon

society in the Middle Ages and immediately subsequent times, must be readily inferred from what has gone before in this very imperfect sketch. We have seen that this institution was the embryo of modern military discipline and tactic, and the beginning of a standing army ; that it afforded a school for the exercise of manly virtue and the formation of refined manners ; that its interior ideal, its primitive mainspring, lay in the normal religiousness of man's nature—an outcome of which was the exaltation of woman. Hallam calls it " the best school of moral discipline of the Middle Ages," and this is high praise from one whom Lord Macaulay calls the least of a worshipper he knew. Still I venture a step farther, and dare to affirm that the pure and simple creed of the mediæval chevalier affords to all ages the best formulation of, and that its pure and simple practice affords the best illustration of, the natural religion of humanity ; and this is as much and something more than a moral discipline. To us moderns,

" Heirs of all the ages, in the foremost files of time,"

a glance backward toward this phenomenon of the times we are accustomed to call dark is, or should be, useful. It is good for us to turn the yellow leaves of time's herbarium and look upon this faded mediæval bloom, howbeit our nineteenth-century hothouse cultures can far outvie the lone wild-flower of the past. We have indeed the needle-gun and *mitrailleuse* where they had lances ; we have churches, one for every dozen worshippers, where they had a dozen monasteries for a nation ; we have schools, one apiece for every boy and girl, where they had one university for an empire ; we have Tyndalls and Huxleys to scatter broadcast

science (exact or otherwise) where kings and scholars in
mediæval times had but the rudiments of each ; we have
Moodys and Sankeys and Salvation Armies where they
had mendicant friars and barefooted pilgrims ; we have
summer schools of philosophy and religion where they had
blind and bloody Crusades ; Swinburnes and Walt Whit-
mans refine and clarify our poetic senses in place of their
rude troubadours and minstrels—all this and immeasurably
more we have in our day over the Sodoms and Gomorrahs
of their day.   And for all this gigantic aggregation of culture, and science, and art—for all the accumulations of these
successive centuries wherein we have

"Ransacked the ages, spoiled the climes,"

how as pigmies to giants, in point of moral altitude, should
most of us compare with these unschooled mediævals !   No
need to make a comment here.   Our morning papers bring
us all we need, with their long, black list of betrayed trusts,
of cowardice, of falsehood, of political intrigue.   And if
the velvet curtain that backgrounds our " best society" but
rise a little, ah me !   what skeletons dance behind the scene !
When in our arrogant nineteenth-century hearts we shall
have fully apprehended the truth that intellectual accumulation is not moral attainment ;   that civilization is not Christianity ;   that culture is not character ;   that, however lit up
by the blazing chandeliers of science, and culture, and art
which swing from our frescoed ceilings in place of that single star of chivalry which beamed down through the rafters
to the mediæval chevalier, we have not, *therefore*, gained
one particle the more illumination of soul—then, indeed,
we shall not disdain to turn our proud faces backward, and

learn how to salt our unsavory knowledge with the wisdom of time's children, the creed of the chevalier !

And while we gain for ourselves one good thing from the backward glance, let us add to it another. While we are learning to respect mediæval humanity, let us try to strengthen our faith in modern humanity as well. In our reaction from our own century, let us not join the ranks of those few eminent persons, and those many persons who desire to be eminent, who seem to find it necessary to do injustice to the present in order to do justice to the past.

Let us not cry with Sir Bedivere :

> " Oh, my Lord Arthur, whither shall I go ?
> Where shall I hide my forehead and my eyes ?
> For now I see the true old times are dead
> When every morning brought a noble chance,
> And every chance brought out a noble knight.
> Such times have been not since the light that led
> The holy elders, with the gift of myrrh.
> But now the whole round table is dissolved
> Which was an image of a mighty world ;
> And I, the last, go forth companionless,
> And the days darken round me and the years
> Among new men, strange faces, other minds."—

But let us answer with Arthur :

> " The old order changeth, yieldeth place to new,
> And God fulfils Himself in many ways,
> Lest one good custom should corrupt the world.
> Comfort thyself—what comfort is in me ?
> I have lived my life, and that which I have done
> May He within Himself make pure !"

Ilium fuit! and Anchises, and Priam, and Hector ! But let us bethink ourselves also that Æneas was, and the Lavi-

nian shores, and the lofty walls of Rome ; and as we look
around us on our Western lands—Lavinian shores on which
many modern knights draw consecrated lances—let us acknowledge that " there is a spirit in man"—man, the man
of Egypt, the man of Hellas, the man of the Tiber, the
man of history, the man of to-day—a spirit breathed into
him with God's own breath, which makes grand and chiv-
alrous deeds possible in every age.

> " Mother Earth ! are the heroes dead ?
>   Do they thrill the soul of the years no more ?
> Are the gleaming snows and the poppies red
>   All that is left of the brave of yore ?
> Are there none to fight as Theseus fought,
>   Far in the young world's misty dawn ?
> Or to teach as the gray haired Nestor taught ?
>   Mother Earth ! are the heroes gone ?
>
> " Gone ?   In a grander form they rise ;
>   Dead ?   We may clasp their hands in ours ;
> And catch the light of their clearer eyes,
>   And wreathe their brows with immortal flowers.
> Wherever a noble deed is done
>   'Tis the pulse of a hero's heart is stirred ;
> Wherever Right has a triumph won
>   There are the heroes' voices heard.
>
> " Their armor rings on a fairer field
>   Than the Greek and the Trojan fiercely trod,
> For Freedom's sword is the blade they wield,
>   And the light above is the smile of God.
> So, in his isle of calm delight,
>   Jason may sleep the years away ;
> For the heroes live, and the sky is bright,
>   And the world is a braver world to-day."

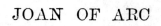

JOAN OF ARC

JOAN OF ARC.

In the century which the year 1428 completed, all the adverse fates had conspired with the Plantagenet purpose to extinguish France. In 1328, at the death of the last Capet, Edward III., of England, rose up before the peers of France with his egregious claim for the French crown. A clever twisting of some loose strands in the cordage of the Salic law served for a pretext to contest his claim against the clearer claim of Philip of Valois. The grandson with his might drew up before the cousin with his right, and then commenced that century of war which made France the bloodless, nerveless thing we find her at this first quarter of the fifteenth century. At Cressy and at Poitiers, and in divers lesser fields, the chivalry of France was mowed by English steel. The frightful horrors of Calais unnerved the nation. And yet, like the heroic citizens of Calais, all France held out against the life-long siege which Edward III. pressed round the kingdom—held out until death conquered the besieger and succored the besieged.

But in this century, between Edward III. of England and Henry V. of England, not war alone, but pestilence and famine—those steadfast handmaids of Bellona—conspired against the life of France. The temple of Janus for one hundred years was not closed, and the box of Pandora discharged itself of every evil on the unhappy

realm.   A pestilence unprecedented in the annals of pesti-
lences, and caused by the presence of so many dead lying
unburied, by reason of the Pope's interdict, in numberless
battle-fields over Europe, swept the south of France, carry-
ing off two out of every three of the inhabitants.   The
shadow of this black death fell everywhere.   Ships rocked
and drifted at sea, unmanned save by this pale pirate, whose
touch had laid crews and passengers lifeless at their posts.

Increasing the terror of the people, a wild fanaticism
became also epidemic.   Bands of half-crazed persons,
clothed in white, wound in and out of the death-darkened
villages of France, beating their breasts and chanting sup-
plications, throwing themselves on the ground, confessing
their sins, and leaving everywhere apprehension and dis-
may, and the echo of their moaning prayer :

> " Nun hebet auf eure Hände
> Dass Gott dies Grosse sterben wende
> Nun hebet auf eure Hände
> Dass sich Gott über uns erbarme !"

These fanatics and others akin to them had great influence
with the people.   And they had the people all to themselves, for the educated clergy stood aloof.

Religion was feeble ; superstition rampant.   The Church
had no coherence ; the state no support.   The kings of
France were beaten, and discrowned, and imprisoned.
Their dukes deserted the royal standard, and made war
among themselves.

The houses of Burgundy and Orleans sent their subtle
foxes running through the land with firebrands of civil
war.   In 1418 a massacre of the Armagnacs by the Bur-

gundians took place in Paris—a massacre without a parallel in all the massacre-filled pages of French history until the Revolution, says Hallam, in spite of St. Bartholomew.

In 1358 the peasantry, stung into self-defence, reared their bruised heads against the oppressive Valois heel with cobra virulence, and the Jacquerie of the fourteenth century of French history set the type for the Jacobins of the eighteenth.

Des Serres thus represents the state of France at the conclusion of this century : " In sooth, the estate of France was most miserable. There appeared nothing but a horrible face, confusion, poverty, desolation, solitarinesse and feare. The lean and bare laborers in the country did terrify even theeves themselves, who had nothing left to spoil but the carkasses of these poor, miserable creatures, wandering up and down like ghosts drawn out of their graves. . . . The least farms and hamlets were fortified by these robbers, English, Bourguignons, and French, every one striving to do his worst ; all men of warre were well agreed to spoile the countryman and the merchant. Even the catell, accustomed to the larume bell, the signe of the enemy's approach, would run home of themselves, without any guide, by this accustomed misery." Petrarch, visiting France in this century, thus describes it : " Nothing presented itself to my eyes but a fearful solitude, an extreme poverty, lands uncultivated, houses in ruins. Even the neighborhood of Paris manifested everywhere marks of destruction and conflagration. The streets are deserted, the roads overgrown with weeds, the whole is a vast solitude." It is said that the city of Paris was so solitary and neglected that in successive years wolves entered the city through the river and devoured and wounded a number of persons.

Thus had the fates conspired with the Plantagenet purpose and prepared the way for Henry V.—a second Edward III.—to propose the treaty which should secure to himself and his posterity the throne of France. With incredible arrogance, in 1420 this great King of England promised an adjustment of all difficulties between France and England upon the basis of the famous treaty of Troyes. He said : " I will take *now* the Princess Catherine for a wife and the regency of France ; and at the death of the king I will succeed to his crown and his kingdom, and join them to my crown and my kingdom, to be mine and my posterity's forever. In return for so much, I will put my sword into the scabbard, and let you, Queen Isabella, have your amours and your intrigues undisturbed, and you, Burgundy, have your vengeance on Orleans, since that serves my cause as well."

With incredible dishonesty the debased queen and remorseless duke signed, over the imbecile old head of Charles VI., the treaty which gave his crown and kingdom to the Plantagenet posterity, and made France a colony of England. With incredible pusillanimity a balance of the peers of France acceded to the treaty. And now, in the year 1420, Henry V. of England is Regent of France, absolute ruler of all the realm north of the Loire. With haughty confidence he awaits the imminent hour when the old baby king shall totter off the stage and leave him, in name, and fame, and full possession, that to which he holds this marvellous title-deed. No matter that this deed is by all law null and void ; no matter that the thing conveyed

was not the property of the conveyors. What the pen has
traced in ink will suffice until the sword can superscribe in
blood ! Might, might ! that is Henry's ; he will make it
right.

Thus two years pass, and in 1422 the prize seems nearer.
" Almost mine !" says the Plantagenet proposer. *"Never
thine,"* says the Divine Disposer. Suddenly, unheralded,
the conqueror of Henry V. rises into view. A pale
cavalier, all unweaponed and unattended, meets him in the
way. No need to call thy mighty men, Plantagenet ! No
need to raise that whetted sword of thine ! No challenge
here to prove thy dauntless courage or thy knightly
courtesy. This battle will be bloodless. This foe is not a
Frenchman. He will say no word, nor urge a claim, nor
draw a sword. He will but look thee in the face, will
beckon thee, will turn his steed, and thou wilt follow him.
And where he leads thou wilt not wear the wedded crown
of France and England ! Well, death thus gives the
unplanned-for cue, and Henry, who would be manager,
makes the first exit. Two months later the summons
comes for Charles, and the old imbecile King of France
totters off the stage. And now we watch for a speedy
dénouement of this dark drama which the adverse fates
have plotted for a hundred years against the realm of
France.

But we watch in vain. The tragedy moves on. When
Henry died he left Plantagenets behind to carry on his *rôle*.
The regent dukes of England unrolled the Troyes treaty
and shook it haughtily, defiantly, in the face of France.
The Duke of Bedford took the paper in one hand and the
infant heir of Henry in the other, and pronounced him at

Paris Henry VI., King of France and England. And all the swords of England stood behind, flanked by Burgundy's steel.

The Dauphin, third son of Charles VI. of France, alike proclaimed, by his few and feeble adherents in the south, King of France, lurked timorously around, fearing the shadow of his royalty. There was no King of France, and there was no France for a king. And so it went for seven years. Henry, King of France, and Charles, King of France, and no France, and no king!

But the fates were brewing, and some shape must soon emerge from out this steaming caldron. One or the other of the contesting forces must prevail, and that right soon.

The odds were fearfully in England's favor. Henry VI. of England was now, though but a child, a king in his own right. His nobility were skilful, and courageous, and ambitious; his yeomanry invincible; his cause so popular that recruits flocked to his standard from every quarter.

Charles VII. of France, in full manhood, was but a child in character—a timorous, self-indulgent trifler, fooling, flirting, feeding in the corner there at Chinon; his forces inadequate, his cavalry thinned by English lances, his peasantry by scythes of pestilence and famine; his only allies Scotchmen, scant and hard to get at any price; his finances so low that no inducement could be offered to the poorest of his subjects in his battle-fields. For the loan of six thousand men Charles offered a province to the King of Scotland. Comines, a historian contemporary with this king, relates how he—the king—having tried on a pair of boots, told the shoemaker that he had no money to pay for them.

But neither loyalty nor royalty compelled the thrifty Crispin to present to his sovereign the necessary boots, or to give him credit for future pay. He chose the safer way, and kept the boots, while His Majesty went slipshod ! With no kingdom, no subjects, no money, no manhood, and—no boots—naught could this little Frenchman do but turn away from such unpleasantness to seek a more congenial programme in the boudoir of Sorel. " Sire," said a courtier to him, " I do not believe it possible that one should lose a kingdom with greater gayety !"

Here, then, is the kingdom of Charlemagne, whose boundaries, six hundred years before, were the Vistula joining the Danube on the east, the Ebro and the Atlantic Ocean on the west, the Mediterranean on the south, the Baltic Sea on the north, reduced to a varying quantity below the river Loire ! " Our Henry V.," boasts Disraeli, " had reduced the kingdom of France to the town of Bourges !"

And thus much only remaining French, what power shall prevent the whole realm from becoming to England what Canada is to-day ? what Cuba is to Spain ?—what power shall arise to preserve for the nineteenth century the French feather of French genius, the bite of French wit, the flavor of French character, the winey *bouquet* of French literature, the *esprit*, the *verve*, the *je ne sais quoi*, all unmatched and unmatchable, unmixed and unmixable, with which France has spiced the world ? Consider the conclusion—how lame, how impotent—had the ether of French intellect become incorporated in the solid fibre of English intellect ! Guizot reduced to Macaulay ; two Carlyles in place of one Carlyle and one Hugo ; two bloody

Marys in place of one bloody Mary and one bloody Medici ;
two Henry VIII.s instead of one great Henry Tudor
and one great Henry Bourbon ; two Marlboroughs instead of one tremendous Marlborough and one tremendous Bonaparte ; two Lady Mary Wortley Montagus instead of one Lady Mary and one De Staël ; all beef—no
poulet! Human nature without the top-dressing of French
nature !

It is the October of the year 1428. Upon the dolorous
disk of France is darkness everywhere, with little difference
in degree. Yet as we strain our vision a deeper shade
blackens in one direction, as if the pall of death were about
there to drop.

The city of Orleans was an ancient stronghold of the
realm. When the King of France was scarcely more than
one among his lords, in the feudal ages of its history,
when, as king, he held two counties, perhaps, when his
lords held one each—himself a count a trifle lordlier than
his subject counts—Orleans was always one of the king's
counties. And the city was the centre of the county.
By this fifteenth century the city of Orleans had acquired
great importance and accumulated great wealth. The city
site was on the north bank of the Loire, but its suburbs
made an annex city—like a Brooklyn to New York—on the
south side. A massive bridge ran across and bound the
two together.

The English, advancing from the north, were building
ponderous bastiles or forts—gigantic posts of a fence to
which their numerous forces were the living rails—around
the land side of the city. This completed, all escape was
made impossible from the north side of the besieged town.

But to preserve means of egress from the city for themselves was less important to the besieged than that the besiegers should lack means of ingress to the city. The Orleanais destroyed the arch that connected the towers on the bridge across to suburban Orleans, and if there was no getting out for the French, neither was there any getting in for the English. But while they thus destroy their southern means of escape, the English are drilling in the last bastile that encloses them upon the north. And now what remains for Orleans but fire, famine, flood, or— surrender? Upon these massive city walls, hoar and honorable, with many a foe resisted since a thousand years and more, when Attila and his terrible Huns hammered on its gates, is written—by no invisible scribe, but with the whetted point of English swords—the *mene, mene* of its doom.

We hear much of the hour and the man. Surely now and here, if ever in history, is the hour. But where is the man ?

The eyes of all men turn to Orleans. Of all men ; but another eye looks down upon another spot, and hither the inexplicable Genius of History bids us go with her.

A strange irrelevance, this scene on which she bids us look ! What can these sloping hills of Domremy, these trilling streams, these low-roofed cottages, have to do with that fated city ? The little shepherd girl who sits beneath the great tree in the doorway yonder, what can her rapt, romantic, saintly face have of importance to thee, O destiny of men and nations ?

But the Genius makes no response except to bid us nearer to these pastoral frivolities, this dreaming shepherd girl.

We see her wander up and down the gentle slopes, peering with eyes that see beyond our vision into the great oak forest, or listening to sounds we cannot hear beneath the fairy tree. We see her spring with lithe, intrepid grace upon the horses of the farm, and mounted, like a soldier, make all the thrusts and passes of a knight preparing for the fray. We see her sitting silent, while her skilful fingers ply her needle at the humble fireside, in that early winter of 1428, listening to tales of the distress of France, the siege of Orleans, the imminent crisis of the kingdom's fate which the roving bands of Charles' adherents bring to Domremy. We see her, "about the hour of noon, in summer-time," in her father's garden, and we see a kindling in that innocent eye, a purpose in that girlish face. And she tells us that a voice of God comes to her, and with the voices a bright light shines. And often she hears the voice and sees the light; and St. Michael, and St. Margaret, and St. Catherine appear to her, in a halo of glory, their heads crowned with jewels, their voices mild and sweet. She hears them when the bells are sounding for the hour of prayer. She hears the voices in the forest also, and at many times and places, and they speak so soothingly that she kneels and weeps because they do not take her with them back to Paradise. But the voices say she must stay and save France from the ruin that impends. And, by and by, when tidings come of the distress of Orleans, of the dauphin's helplessness, of the invincible strength of the English, of the swift approach to Orleans of doom from which there is none to deliver in all that stricken realm, the voices bid her *up!* and herself go forth to rescue France!

And while we curl our lips at this wild ranting of the half-mad shepherd girl and turn to go our way to Orleans, where the hour wanes and all hearts wait, with hope against hope, for the man—the hand of destiny unclasps from ours, and, with inexorable finger, points to the girlish figure, and amid the protests of our impatient scorn we hear the voice that none may question saying to her: *"Thou art the man!"*

It is the 25th of April, 1429. The pall is just about to drop on Orleans. An instant yet remains before the English have filled in the last rail to the living fence which bristles round the place ; an instant ere the last Plantagenet sword is wedged into the last loophole of escape ; an instant of the hour yet awaits the coming of the man. The beats of time strike like funeral peals and chime with the heart-throbs of the Orleanais. French breaths are held and French arms are paralyzed with fear. Even little King Charles, the spaniel, trips it heavily behind the skirts of Agnes Sorel, in his squalid little court at Chinon.

As we gaze upon the scene in this moment of suspense, while the darkness deepens to extinction—in the very article of fatal asphyxia—the wondrous transformation comes. The peerless panoramist slides suddenly before us the next scene in the spectacle—a scene we all know well.

We saw that shining face lifted to the skies of Domremy. We behold that slight, intrepid figure, mounted now upon a fiery war-horse, wielding now a glittering sword. It is the little peasant maid who wears that fifty pounds of burnished steel with such a knightly grace. The head is without helmet, and the raven ringlets float out to the air : the face, uncovered, reveals the same rapt countenance, upon the battle-field, we saw beneath the tree within the door-yard. We all behold that gorgeous banner of white satin strewn with the French lilies, on which the figure of a conqueror in glory shines, above the words which flame beneath, *Jésus Maria !* This held in one of those girlish hands, and in the other the consecrated lance, marked with the crosses of St. Catherine. We all know the doer and the deed ! No need to tell the oft-told tale, which set forth in the soberest hues of fact, yet seems to waking sense most like a wildest dream of fancy ; no need to repeat the story of the old chronicler Hall—the English historian of that day—who tells how " Pucelle, with French capitaine, in the dedde tyme of ye night, and in a great rayne and thundere, entered into the citie." We all know what followed on this entrance, which the Duke of Bedford thus reports to his sovereign, Henry VI.:

" There felle, by the hand of God, as it scemeth, a grete stroke upon your people that was there (before Orleans) assembled, in grete nombre, caused, in grete partie, as of trowe of lakke of sadde beleve and of unlevefulle doubt that they hadde of a disciple and lyme of the Feende called the Pucelle, that used fals enchantments and sorcerie."

We all know how the little King Charles, the spaniel, trotted forth to Rheims, and with royal condescension took from the peasant girl the crown and throne of France ; we all know how this little hand of muckle might, laid on the rusty crank, set in swift revolution the wheel of France's fortune ; how the treacherous Burgundy turned from his allegiance with the English and returned to stand by Charles ; how thus the left hand clasped the right and grew again to the dismembered body of the empire ; how that empire convalesced and grew to giant stature in the years to come.

Had I the ability to narrate the story of Joan of Arc worthily, I could scarcely have the heart to add one more to the long list of poems, and romances, and histories which, from a Shakespeare, a Southey, and a Schiller, to the prize essayists and the undergraduates, have accumulated since the fifteenth century. Yet had I such desire, it could not take much time or great space to tell the round, unvarnished tale. Unassisted by tradition, stripped of romance and invention, we find that a few simple pictures make the panorama of her life. A little peasant maiden doing lowly service in the cottage home at Domremy ; a mail-clad maiden leading forth her soldiers from the gates of Orleans—two faithful feet on fagots at Rouen—a radiant face uplifted to the beckoning skies—a crucifix upheld in shrivelling, flame-kissed hands—a wreath of smoke for shroud, a wrack of smoke for pall, a heap of ashes, and—a franchised soul !

There is no figure in history more incendiary to the imagination than this of Joan of Arc—not one which more enlists the energies of the Philistine, approaching us from every quarter with demands that we subdue to the substantial hues of the historic imagination, this tale, which we are predestined by him to invest with the ethereal tints of the poetic imagination. The Philistine's error is always in his premises. His conclusions are unassailable, always logical, therefore always wrong, because founded upon wrong premises. He frowns down the story of Joan because it shines and glows in rose-color. His error is in denying to history any rose-color. He starts with the premise that rose-color is of no use, and ends with the conclusion that there are no roses.

Now, a rose would smell as sweet by any other name, simply because it must still remain a rose. And a rose has its rights as well as a cabbage. The cabbage-growers say it does not pay as well as cabbage, but all the same the rose is red, and sweet, and immortal! A true story of the Maid of Orleans will take away many accessories with which the poets have invested her, but she must still remain a glowing rose in history, fair and immortal. We welcome the Philistine when he brings us words like these :

"It is the business of history to distinguish between the miraculous and the marvellous ; to reject the first in all narrations merely profane or human ; to doubt the second ; and when obliged by unquestionable testimony, as in the present case, to admit of something extraordinary, to receive as little of it as is consistent with the known facts and circumstances."

Good, Mr. Hume! We are to reject the miraculous, to doubt the marvellous, and to receive only as little of the extraordinary as the known facts and circumstances compel us to! Very good. And now, Mr. Hume, for your definitions.

Define for us the miraculous. Define for us the marvellous. And when you have given us perfect definitions of these two, then we will reject the one and doubt the other, and accept only the extraordinary!

Meanwhile we find to our purpose certain words of old Bishop Butler, who had somewhat to say of the extraordinary. "There are two courses," he said, "of nature. One is the ordinary, the other the *extraordinary*." It is this extraordinary course of nature which produces those phenomena which, being out of the common, are out of our sphere, and therefore which we are accustomed to call supernatural—or superhuman—a miracle, or a marvel. Yet they are necessarily neither, but only extraordinary courses of nature, outside of our knowledge of law, yet not, therefore, outside the sphere of law. What is law? Trace it link by link, pursue it phase by phase, chase its shadow until you find its substance, and what—*who* have you found? You have found *God*.

Resolve the supernatural. Find that which is above nature. Take your line and measure nature, that you may define her limits. Sweep your arc until it is a circumscribing circumference, so that you may perceive that which is the above-nature, the beyond-nature. What is the measure of your measure? What is the radius of your circumference? Nature, nature! What have you outside? What is there that bears not the image and superscription, in its phase ordinary, or its phase extraordinary, of the Cæsar of the universe? Who is above this Cæsar? Who but her maker—God? He who fills nature and who is nature alone exceeds nature, and is that which nature is not. What is a miracle? What is a marvel? A miracle is that which comes about by processes *outside the sphere of our observation*. It is a phenomenon which is the product of that working of law which is *beyond our knowledge of its working*. Shall we call it therefore a phenomenon outside of the working of law? It is a result from that course of nature which is extraordinary. Shall we therefore call it supernatural? Lamartine says of Joan of Arc: "Everything in her life seems miraculous, and yet the miracle is not in her voice, her vision, her sign, her standard, or her

sword, but in herself." And yet I should say, least of all,
"in herself."

Nay, let us reject the miraculous theory of Joan of Arc.
Let us reject the marvellous. Let us cling to and claim for
her only the extraordinary. For in her I, for my part, see
no nature which I do not see in many a woman of to-day ;
but the exercise of that nature we do not often see. What,
then, were the " courses of nature" which in her could
produce the " extraordinary" ?

I reduce all the miracle, and marvel, and mystery of
Joan's history to the extraordinary development of one
human capacity—love ; the extraordinary exercise of one
human capacity—faith.

Joan's love was extraordinary because it was not a passion
for a person, but a quenchless passion of love for a cause.
All the energy, and devotion, and credulity, and constancy,
and jealousy, and consuming passion, and triumphant worship that goes into a woman's love for one man, and that
makes it the thing it is, went from Joan's soul into the
cause of France. All that a woman will endure for and from
her lover or her child, that did Joan endure for and from
France. And this is very extraordinary ; strange and rare
in man—stranger and rarer in woman. And Joan's faith
was extraordinary—as is all faith, since it is from God—a
gift rather than a grace. To Joan man was as naught ; the
King of France was the vicar of Heaven. The little "*King
of Bourges*" was one whom God had appointed governor
over this, His kingdom, France. She, Joan, was a messenger, a missionary. Faith fused at once into obedience.
How extraordinary, how simple ! In this scientific age—
this age of iconoclasm—it is greatly good for us to confront

things rich, rare, out-of-the-common—things above our power to comprehend, beyond our power to destroy. It is well for us who are so blind to the rose-color in our daily lives to be forced to acknowledge its existence in the imperishable canvas of history ; well for us, so intensely practical as we are, to be compelled there, at least, to confront the romantic and the heroic. So only perhaps can we be made to believe in the possible heroic of to-day.

For the enduring quality in this wondrous figure of the centuries is the common quality. If I know anything for certain of the individual Joan, it is only because I know something for certain of her sisters of to-day. I see, indeed, in her some characteristics of her age which must tinge her character, and which, not being characteristics of our age, cannot tinge ours. The monstrous superstitions of her times are broken bubbles of thin air in our agnostic century. The dense ignorance of her day cannot be repeated in any after-time. The blind fanaticism of that age is wholly fled. And yet, superstition, ignorance, fanaticism, remain ; and unless we can share in this our luminous century that one priceless gift of God, which in this poor shepherd girl, along with her ignorance, and superstition, and fanaticism, was her power, and must be our power, if we have any,—then we may well put this complex age, full of knowledge and discovery, into the balance against that age, and watch in vain for any turning of the scales in our favor. Faith ! Faith ! that was Joan's lever—the lever by which that little hand moved the world—literally moved the world, for Orleans was France, and England was the world. Let no one dream that Joan was very clever ; let no one dream that she had military genius.

Her power was but the power which many another woman may have—the power of a buoyant, masterful faith in God, in herself, in humanity, *and a will to come to the rescue.* It is good to make acquaintance with her—with *her*, not with some wretched travesty of her. For in her we contemplate not military genius, not surpassing cleverness, not superhuman wisdom ; but we do, if we will, contemplate goodness and purity. And within the folds of these incontestable facts we may behold this shining truth : that, when the soul is possessed by a great purpose, all small and minor purposes are lost ; that the woman-soul, when in faith it sets itself to come to the rescue —in church, state, society, family—will subordinate all other things ; and that the citadel of the soul being beforehand possessed of this divine passion to help, all other and selfisher passions will find no admittance.

We can no one of us afford to count the story of Joan of Arc an idle tale. Let what archives will be opened to contradict or alter dates, detail, irrelevant fact—the essential truth which Joan's life stands for, the character which Joan's career reveals, remain unaltered and unalterable, of far greater significance to us as spiritual truth than as the historical fact. Joan of Arc saved France indeed, and raised the siege of Orleans ; but this is not all her immortality. She has entered as a spiritual force into inheritance of the ages, and become a practical influence in human lives. If you and I are not actually helped by this influence, it is our fault, not hers.

For each of us there waits an Orleans. Some time that crisis-battle must be fought which gives us final victory or ultimate defeat. In that long siege which precedes that crisis-battle, we need the faith of Joan, that faith which ranges the soul on the side of the conquering powers, and enlists it in a service which is sure to win. And we need to see our visions, to hear our voices, as did Joan hers ; those visions which open to us from the summits of our holiest resolve, our highest endeavor, our most painful abnegation ; those voices which lay on us most strenuous commands and whisper to us, in secret chambers of our beleaguered souls, words of conviction, of courage, and of cheer. God grant that we be not unresponsive to that angel voice, that we be not disobedient unto the heavenly vision !

Printed in the United Kingdom
by Lightning Source UK Ltd.
100435UKS00001B/18